WHERE IS GOD WHEN...

Joey O'Connor

OLIVER
NELSON

**THOMAS NELSON
PUBLISHERS**
Nashville

Published in Nashville, Tennessee, by Oliver-Nelson Books, a division of Thomas Nelson, Inc., Publishers, and distributed in Canada by Word Communications, Ltd., Richmond, British Columbia.

The Bible version used in this publication is THE NEW KING JAMES VERSION. Copyright © 1979, 1980, 1982, Thomas Nelson, Inc., Publishers.

Library of Congress Cataloging-in-Publication Data

O'Connor, Joey, 1964–
    Where is God when— / Joey O'Connor.
        p. cm.
    ISBN 0-8407-9184-4 (pbk.)
    1. Church work with teenagers.   2. Teenagers—Religious life—Miscellanea.
3. Theology, Doctrinal—Popular works.   4. Theology, Doctrinal—Miscellanea.
I. Title.
BV4447.O25   1993
    248.8'3—dc20
                                                        93–17942
                                                             CIP
                                                              AC

Printed in the United States of America.

1 2 3 4 5 6 — 98 97 96 95 94 93

This book is dedicated to all the staff and students (past and present) at Coast Hills Community Church in Aliso Viejo, California. Your laughter, encouragement, and desire "To Know Christ and Make Him Known" have nurtured and helped shape me into who I am today. It's my prayer that the promises of God's Word enrich your life as much as you have mine.

Special thanks to Dad and Mom, Todd Temple, Jim Burns, Jim Grindle, Denny Bellesi, and most of all, my beautiful bride, Krista, for your unconditional love and belief in me.

CONTENTS

INTRODUCTION

WHERE IS GOD? Is He close by or far away? If you're like most young people, you've probably wondered, *Where is God when I need Him most?*

If God is really God, He could be in all sorts of places. Your bedroom. Dad's tool chest. Third period auto shop. Burkina Faso on the western side of Africa. Your best friend's belly button. The North Pole with Santa Claus. If God is really who He says He is, then He can be anyplace He wants to be. Wouldn't it be great to be God? No calling home. No checking with Mom and Dad. No curfew.

People, young and old alike, wonder where God is because they're searching for Him. Some people won't admit they're actually searching for Him, so instead they say, "I'm searching for peace." Or "I'm trying to discover how to live a happy life." Or "I'm looking for hope." I think everyone, at one time or another, has asked, "Where is God? Does He even exist?" Most people really want to know where God is, especially when they're about to die.

If your life were threatened with immediate pain or possible death, who would you yell for? Mom? Emergency 911? Batman? Your best friend? Or would you yell for God? If most of us were really honest, we wouldn't say we don't believe in God. We'd just like to know where to find Him when we're in a pinch.

You may ask, "Where is God when . . ?" because you're looking for answers to this confusing life and its problems Your problems may not be life-threatening, but they may threaten you in other ways. When you have a problem that's bothering you and there's no one to help you, who do you turn to? When all other options have been exhausted, what do you do?

The One who is available and waiting to listen to you at any moment is God. God isn't as complicated or distant as you may think. God listens to what's on your heart and mind. And He speaks to you through His Word, the Bible. The Bible is like a long love letter written to you so that you can discover how to have a relationship with God. A friendship with your Creator. The result of that relationship is an incredible sense of awe, peace, freedom, happiness, and hope.

God wants you to know more about Him and what He is like. By having a relationship with Jesus Christ, you can understand who God is. Here are some BIG words in simple, user-friendly language that will help you understand more about God:

- *Omnipresent.* From Mars to Madagascar, God is everywhere. He cannot be limited to a location or place. That means He can help you wherever you are.
- *Omnipotent.* God can F-L-E-X. He's All-Powerful, All-World, and All-Universe when it comes to being strong and making the impossible possible.
- *Omniscient.* You could call God smart, intelligent, a brain, or a know-it-all because that's what He is. There is no secret, wonder, mystery, idea, math problem, thought, or question that is hidden to Him or that He doesn't already have the answer to.
- *Sovereign.* Kings, presidents, dictators, and rulers will come and go, but God is the supreme ruler over everything. For those who trust and love Him, He promises to work all problems toward good and not harm.
- *Eternal.* You can have hope in God and in His eternal presence because He promises that He will always be with you. He'll never leave you, forsake you, drop you off, kick you out, or tell you to take a hike.
- *Immutable.* God never changes. He's always the same. He isn't

affected by moods, atmospheric conditions, or tidal changes. God is perfect. He will always help you, understand you, love you, and promise to walk with you, no matter how difficult a problem becomes.

- *Infinite*. God is beyond limitations, measurements, sizes, and conceptions. God's infinite and powerful presence in your life can shake out depression, pain, and sorrow.

This book is written to help you discover God and what He has to say in His Word for whatever problem, conflict, disaster, frustration, question, or situation you may have. For every situation you encounter, God's promises are always with you. God's Word always tells us to confront and deal with problems and never to run away from them. When you read a verse in this book, look it up in your Bible so you can discover the context in which it's written. Ask yourself when you're reading, How can what I'm reading help me to better know and love God so I can serve Him in every area of my life? If you have further questions, talk to your parents, youth pastor, church leader, or friend. Study God's Word responsibly. He gave it to us to accomplish His purposes.

Chapter ONE

A True Original

BEFORE I MARRIED, my friends and I headed to Santa Barbara one weekend to surf and visit friends in college. After a great surf session on a beautiful Saturday morning, we went to a local restaurant for breakfast. A pretty young woman at the table next to us caught my eye. She looked familiar, but I couldn't place where I had seen her before. A full-length cast covered her left leg. She sat by herself looking at some slides. Where have I seen her before? I kept asking myself.

Aha! It finally came to me. Trying to be very cool about it, I whispered to my friends, "Dana! Bobby! Look who's sitting at the table behind you. It's Kathy Ireland!"

Bobby and Dana looked to see if it was true. "I don't know, Joey. Are you sure?" Bobby asked.

"Yes, I'm sure. Look, she even has slides from a photo shoot."

Sure enough, as we were debating back and forth whether or not she was the Kathy Ireland of *Sports Illustrated* fame, two of her friends arrived at her table and said, "Hi, Kathy! How's it going? Are those new photos of you?"

Every day hundreds of thousands of young people gape at the high-paid models in modern fashion, muscle, and fitness magazines. Billions of dollars are spent each year in advertising to woo you into buying whatever's being served up in the latest cosmopolitan cafeteria of creature comforts.

Being consumed with buying the newest line of clothes or wearing the latest hairstyles can cause us to forget that we are true originals. God's originals. When we forget that we are "fearfully and wonderfully made" (Psalm 139:14), three things can happen.

1. *We begin to believe that outer beauty is more important than inner beauty.* Television, movies, and magazines constantly bombard us with the message that we don't measure up. We're defined by what we look like. The One who made you to be a true original says something completely different: "The LORD does not see as man sees; for man looks at the outward appearance, but the LORD looks at the heart" (1 Samuel 16:7).

2. *We play the Comparison Game.* We've all played it at one time or another. My pastor explains the Comparison Game like this: "When you compare yourself to others, you make yourself superior or inferior to the other person. And neither of these two things is a godly characteristic."

3. *We copy others.* If everyone tries to copy everyone else, nobody's an original. God has gifted you with your own mind, thoughts, feelings, and personality. *There is no one else like you! You are a true original!*

A Big, Fat, Selfish Pig

(Selfishness)

When I was a senior in high school, I had a fetal pig named Piggy Sue. My anatomy and physiology teacher gave her to me, and I kept her in our refrigerator at home. Over the course of the semester, I learned quite a bit about pigs. But there was one thing about pigs I didn't understand. A friend had told me pigs don't sweat, they wallow. At the time I didn't know what he meant.

But since then, I've learned why pigs wallow in the mud. Pigs aren't born with sweat glands. Unlike humans, pigs can't sweat. To keep from overheating and exploding sausage and bacon all over the place, pigs roll around in the mud to cool themselves.

Humans are a lot like swine. Just as it is a pig's nature to wallow, it is our nature to be self-centered. We don't have it in us to be natural givers. We are selfish. We do what the Bible calls sin. God's Word helps us become more like His Son Jesus and less like animals that wallow. He gives us a completely new nature in Christ. When we wallow in ourselves, we give off an odor that repels others. That stinks. But if we live in the new nature God gives us, we probably won't act quite like pigs.

Where is God when I want more and more "stuff"? How can I stop being so materialistic?

Incline my heart to Your testimonies, and not to covetousness (Psalm 119:36).

Where is God when I try to make myself look better than others, but I end up looking worse?

Let nothing be done through selfish ambition or conceit, but in lowliness of mind let each esteem others better than himself (Philippians 2:3).

Where is God when I lend money to someone who doesn't repay me?

And if you lend to those from whom you hope to receive back, what credit is that to you? For even sinners lend to sinners to receive as much back But love your enemies, do good, and lend, hoping for nothing in return; and your reward will be great, and you will be sons of the Most High (Luke 6:34–35).

Where is God when I resent friends who get all the lucky breaks?

But if you have bitter envy and self-seeking in your hearts, do not boast and lie against the truth (James 3:14).

Where is God when I feel like a slave to selfishness?

Knowing this, that our old man was crucified with Him, that the body of sin might be done away with, that we should no longer be slaves of sin. For he who has died has been freed from sin (Romans 6:6–7).

Where is God when my friends and I try to outdo each other and our friendship suffers because of it?
For where envy and self-seeking exist, confusion and every evil thing are there (James 3:16).

Where is God when my selfishness gets in the way of following Jesus?
Then He said to them all, "If anyone desires to come after Me, let him deny himself, and take up his cross daily, and follow Me" (Luke 9:23).

Where is God when I'm sick of myself and the way I act?
That you put off, concerning your former conduct, the old man which grows corrupt according to the deceitful lusts, and be renewed in the spirit of your mind, and that you put on the new man which was created according to God, in true righteousness and holiness (Ephesians 4:22–24).

Crunching Out Conformity

(Being God's Person)

A challenge you face as a teenager is to conform your life to God's standards or to the world's standards. God wants to transform your life so you can be the unique person He meant for you to be. But the world wants to press you into a cookie-cutter mold.

Fear of discovering who you are can cause you to conform to who you think others are. But how can you be sure others know who they really are? If they are trying to be like everybody else, they won't have a clue about their true selves. (UGH!)

In the book of Galatians, Paul told how he was transformed in Jesus Christ: "I have been crucified with Christ; it is no longer I who live, but Christ lives in me; and the life which I now live in the flesh I live by faith in the Son of God, who loved me and gave Himself for me" (Galatians 2:20). Paul understood that God made him to be like no one else but Christ. Is that conformity? Yes. Is that meaningless? No. Developing and growing in a friendship with Jesus Christ can help you discover who you are in God's family.

Where is God when I change my appearance to fit in with the crowd, but I still feel like an outsider?

And do not be conformed to this world, but be transformed by the renewing of your mind, that you may prove what is that good and acceptable and perfect will of God (Romans 12:2).

Where is God when I'm often tempted to dump Him and go back to my old ways?

As obedient children, not conforming yourselves to the former lusts, as in your ignorance (1 Peter 1:14).

Where is God when I can't understand why so many of my Christian friends have fallen away from Him?

For men will be lovers of themselves, lovers of money, boasters, proud, blasphemers, disobedient to parents, unthankful, unholy, unloving, unforgiving, slanderers, without self-control, brutal, despisers of good, traitors, headstrong, haughty, lovers of pleasure rather than lovers of God (2 Timothy 3:2–4).

Where is God when it's easy for me to conform to what others want because I'm not sure if God likes me?

Behold, God is mighty, but despises no one; He is mighty in strength of understanding (Job 36:5).

Where is God when I get impatient waiting for Him to finish what He started in my life?

The LORD will perfect that which concerns me; Your mercy, O LORD, endures forever; do not forsake the works of Your hands (Psalm 138:8).

Where is God when I know I'm supposed to conform my life to His plan, but how do I know He has a purpose for my life?

For it is God who works in you both to will and to do for His good pleasure (Philippians 2:13).

Where is God when I need His strength to help me not go along with the bad things my friends want to do?
Therefore we also pray always for you that our God would count you worthy of this calling, and fulfill all the good pleasure of His goodness and the work of faith with power (2 Thessalonians 1:11).

Where is God when I'm afraid of what my friends would think if I really made up my mind to follow Christ?
Nevertheless even among the rulers many believed in Him, but because of the Pharisees they did not confess Him, lest they should be put out of the synagogue; for they loved the praise of men more than the praise of God (John 12:42–43).

Where is God when I need the Holy Spirit's power to help me live by God's ways?
So then, those who are in the flesh cannot please God. But you are not in the flesh but in the Spirit, if indeed the Spirit of God dwells in you (Romans 8:8–9).

Excepting Yourself

(Self-Acceptance)

Accepting yourself for who you are is pretty hard to do if you don't know who you are in the first place. What if you found out who you really were, only to be disappointed?

Many students have no problem accepting who their friends are. But they make an exception when it comes to accepting themselves.

Accept. Except. How can two words sound so similar, yet be continents apart in meaning? According to the *American Heritage Dictionary* (you have one, don't you?), to *accept* means to "receive gladly." To *except* means to "exclude or leave out." Do you exclude yourself more often than you gladly receive the person God has made you to be? With God, there are no exceptions.

Where is God when I have a problem accepting myself and others?
Therefore receive one another, just as Christ also received us, to the glory of God (Romans 15:7).

Where is God when I wonder if people in the Bible ever felt rejected by Him?
For You are the God of my strength; why do You cast me off? Why do I go mourning because of the oppression of the enemy? Oh, send out Your light and Your truth! Let them lead me; let them bring me to Your holy hill and to Your tabernacle (Psalm 43:2-3).

Where is God when I feel rejected and unloved?
Blessed be God, who has not turned away my prayer, nor His mercy from me! (Psalm 66:20).

Where is God when I want to know if Jesus ever got rejected as I do?
And He began to teach them that the Son of Man must suffer many things, and be rejected by the elders and chief priests and scribes, and be killed, and after three days rise again (Mark 8:31).

Where is God when I feel I don't have much to offer Him?
You whom I have taken from the ends of the earth, and called from its farthest regions, and said to you, "You are My servant, I have chosen you and have not cast you away" (Isaiah 41:9).

Where is God when I hate myself because I'm such a geek? Did Jesus ever feel different from everyone else like I do?
He is despised and rejected by men, a Man of sorrows and acquainted with grief. And we hid, as it were, our faces from Him; He was despised, and we did not esteem Him (Isaiah 53:3).

Where is God when I need to know that He accepts me just as I am?

I will strengthen the house of Judah, and I will save the house of Joseph. I will bring them back, because I have mercy on them. They shall be as though I had not cast them aside; for I am the LORD their God, and I will hear them (Zechariah 10:6).

Where is God when people at school reject me? How can I know God won't reject me?
Coming to Him as to a living stone, rejected indeed by men, but chosen by God and precious, you also, as living stones, are being built up a spiritual house, a holy priesthood, to offer up spiritual sacrifices acceptable to God through Jesus Christ (1 Peter 2:4–5).

Monkey See, Monkey Do

(Negative Thoughts)

Have you ever been to the monkey exhibit at the zoo? These crazy primates seem to have as much fun staring at us as we do staring at them. They entertain us by swinging and screeching from tree to tree, then they pause and look us over for a while, chattering among themselves. It makes you wonder who's laughing at who.

Our thoughts are a lot like monkeys staring back at us. They can keep to themselves, or they can torment us with their antics. Jumping up and down in the brain, screeching and fighting, they can wreak havoc on our self-image. Their shrill screams can make us cringe. God can silence the monkeys in your brain by replacing your anxious thoughts with His peace.

Where is God when I need Him to help me clear my thoughts?
Give ear to my prayer, O God, and do not hide Yourself from my supplication. Attend to me, and hear me; I am restless in my complaint, and moan noisily (Psalm 55:1–2).

Where is God when I wonder if He really knows what I'm thinking?

You know my sitting down and my rising up; You understand my thought afar off (Psalm 139:2).

Where is God when I want to please Him by thinking good thoughts and not bad ones?
The thoughts of the wicked are an abomination to the LORD, but the words of the pure are pleasant (Proverbs 15:26).

Where is God when my thoughts toward others aren't very nice, but I want to change?
Let the wicked forsake his way, and the unrighteous man his thoughts; let him return to the LORD, and He will have mercy on him; and to our God, for He will abundantly pardon (Isaiah 55:7).

Where is God when I want to know why some people never think about Him?
The wicked in his proud countenance does not seek God; God is in none of his thoughts (Psalm 10:4).

Where is God when I can't understand what's on His mind? Why doesn't the Bible talk about the way God thinks?
"For My thoughts are not your thoughts, nor are your ways My ways," says the LORD. "For as the heavens are higher than the earth, so are My ways higher than your ways, and My thoughts than your thoughts" (Isaiah 55:8–9).

Where is God when my mind gets bombarded with all sorts of bad thoughts?
Therefore, holy brethren, partakers of the heavenly calling, consider the Apostle and High Priest of our confession, Christ Jesus (Hebrews 3:1).

Where is God when I want to know how to apply God's Word to what goes through my mind?
Therefore you shall lay up these words of mine in your heart and in your soul, and bind them as a sign on your hand, and they shall be as frontlets between your eyes (Deuteronomy 11:18).

Where is God when all my thoughts are selfish and I totally leave Him out? How can I include God in what I'm thinking?

Set your mind on things above, not on things on the earth (Colossians 3:2).

No Comparison

(Comparing Yourself to Others)

Comparing product components or ingredients is important when you have to choose between two similar products. Like Spam and headcheese. I know it's tough deciding between the two, but you need to compare the ingredients lest you buy the less nutritious of the two. Gag!

Comparing products is smart when you're shopping. But comparing yourself to other people is senseless. Why? Because you come out better than or worse than the other guy. Neither way is God's way. Each way creates pride, jealousy, envy, and a poor self-image. There's always going to be someone smarter, funnier, or stronger than you are. If there's one comparison you can make, compare yourself to Jesus. He'll make you to be all that you feel you're not. In shopping, comparison saves. In relationships, comparison kills.

Where is God when I compare myself to others and come out the loser?
For we dare not class ourselves or compare ourselves with those who commend themselves. But they, measuring themselves by themselves, and comparing themselves among themselves, are not wise (2 Corinthians 10:12).

Where is God when I feel worthless?
But the very hairs of your head are all numbered. Do not fear therefore; you are of more value than many sparrows (Luke 12:7).

Where is God when my best friend competes with me, but I don't want to fall into the same trap?
See that no one renders evil for evil to anyone, but always pursue what is good both for yourselves and for all (1 Thessalonians 5:15).

Where is God when I get my priorities mixed up? What can I do?
But seek first the kingdom of God and His righteousness, and all these things shall be added to you (Matthew 6:33).

Where is God when I wrestle with what's more important: inner beauty or outer beauty?
Do not let your adornment be merely outward—arranging the hair, wearing gold, or putting on fine apparel—rather let it be the hidden person of the heart, with the incorruptible beauty of a gentle and quiet spirit, which is very precious in the sight of God (1 Peter 3:3–4).

Where is God when my rich friends tease a kid who doesn't have much money?
He who despises his neighbor sins; but he who has mercy on the poor, happy is he (Proverbs 14:21).

Where is God when I easily give in to the comparison trap?
Be sober, be vigilant; because your adversary the devil walks about like a roaring lion, seeking whom he may devour (1 Peter 5:8).

Where is God when I've got a friend who's nervous about what others think of her?
Anxiety in the heart of man causes depression, but a good word makes it glad (Proverbs 12:25).

Personal Choices

(Making Good Decisions)

"It's my choice. I have the right to do anything I want!" This attitude runs rampant through our country like beavers at a lumber sale. Some people want to do their own thing regardless of how it affects others. They want rights without responsibility, choices without consequences, freedom without faithfulness. People seem to have forgotten that their decisions have a powerful impact on the lives of others.

The prophet Hosea wept when he saw all the cursing, lying, and bloodshed in his country. No one wanted to know God. The people wanted their rights, choices, and personal freedoms at the cost of their faith.

Before making choices, think about a couple of things. First, God has a heart. When you make choices that distance you from God, you hurt yourself, and you hurt God. Second, think about others. What about your family? Would your choices embarrass them? What about your friends? Would your choices hurt them in any way?

It's hard to make good choices if you view God like a judge ready to clobber you with a galaxy gavel. But if you know God as a close friend, Someone who really cares about you, good choices deepen that friendship.

Where is God when I wonder why I should keep following Christ?

Therefore choose life, that both you and your descendants may live; that you may love the LORD your God, that you may obey His voice, and that you may cling to Him, for He is your life (Deuteronomy 30:19–20).

Where is God when it's easy for me to get pulled away from Him because I'm so materialistic?

Receive my instruction, and not silver, and knowledge rather than choice gold (Proverbs 8:10).

Where is God when I wonder if He tempts me to see whether I'll choose to do the right thing or not?

Let no one say when he is tempted, "I am tempted by God"; for God cannot be tempted by evil, nor does He Himself tempt anyone. But each one is tempted when he is drawn away by his own desires and enticed (James 1:13–14).

Where is God when I get so frustrated trying to choose between right and wrong?

For I know that in me (that is, in my flesh) nothing good dwells; for to will is present with me, but how to perform what is good I do not find (Romans 7:18).

Where is God when I need to be encouraged to keep following His ways and not my own?
Yes, in the way of Your judgments, O LORD, we have waited for You; the desire of our soul is for Your name and for the remembrance of You (Isaiah 26:8).

Where is God when I've tried drugs, alcohol, and sexual relationships, but now that I've chosen to follow Christ, everything else pales in comparison?
Whom have I in heaven but You? And there is none upon earth that I desire besides You (Psalm 73:25).

Where is God when I've been hanging out with people known for making trouble, but they don't seem so bad to me?
Do not be envious of evil men, nor desire to be with them (Proverbs 24:1).

Where is God when I really want to put Him first in making good decisions?
I delight to do Your will, O my God, and Your law is within my heart (Psalm 40:8).

Where is God when it seems that the only person I can turn to is Jesus?
Then Jesus said to the twelve, "Do you also want to go away?" But Simon Peter answered Him, "Lord, to whom shall we go? You have the words of eternal life" (John 6:67–68).

When I'm Weak, Then I'm Strong

(Strength in Weakness)

Weakness isn't something that our society holds in high regard. Images of being picked on by bullies and looking like a geek are the subjects of old comic books. It's not cool to cry or show how you really feel in today's world. At school, you've got to appear cool, composed, and totally with it to make it in the eyes of others. When you've got a problem, how can you drop your guard and let others see you're hurting?

It takes guts to be honest and risk being weak when others may not understand. But Jesus understands what it's like being weak. Jesus made Himself to be weak regardless of what others thought of Him. That was pretty risky. When His friend Lazarus died, Jesus wept. When He was bummed out, He took time away from others to pray. Jesus understood the weakness of human beings because He understood the effects of sin. Sin makes us weak, and that's why He came to die for us. He made Himself weak so that we could be strong in Him.

Where is God when I feel so lame that I don't know how to pray better?

Likewise the Spirit also helps in our weaknesses. For we do not know what we should pray for as we ought, but the Spirit Himself makes intercession for us with groanings which cannot be uttered (Romans 8:26).

Where is God when my friends say that it's foolish to believe in God?

Because the foolishness of God is wiser than men, and the weakness of God is stronger than men (1 Corinthians 1:25).

Where is God when I wonder if Paul ever felt scared as a Christian?

I was with you in weakness, in fear, and in much trembling (1 Corinthians 2:3).

Where is God when I am overwhelmed trying to be a good Christian? Does God accept my weaknesses?

Therefore most gladly I will rather boast in my infirmities, that the power of Christ may rest upon me (2 Corinthians 12:9).

Where is God when I make so many mistakes that I feel like I'm bugging Him by asking for forgiveness?
Iniquities prevail against me; as for our transgressions, You will provide atonement for them (Psalm 65:3).

Where is God when I want to know if He understands my weaknesses and will give me power to overcome them?
For though He was crucified in weakness, yet He lives by the power of God. For we also are weak in Him, but we shall live with Him by the power of God toward you (2 Corinthians 13:4).

Where is God when I feel like I'm slipping away from Him?
He can have compassion on those who are ignorant and going astray, since he himself is also subject to weakness (Hebrews 5:2).

Where is God when I get involved in situations way over my head? Will He help me?
With Him are wisdom and strength, He has counsel and understanding (Job 12:13).

Where is God when I've heard all there is to hear about being a Christian, but I want to see it in action?
For the kingdom of God is not in word but in power (1 Corinthians 4:20).

Where is God when I wonder if it's His power or my power that keeps me walking with Him?
But we have this treasure in earthen vessels, that the excellence of the power may be of God and not of us (2 Corinthians 4:7).

A True Original Test

You're truly an original, but do you believe it? Take a few minutes to complete these exercises to discover how God has made no other like you.

1. Write the name of someone who is physically identical to you. (Note: Identical twins can skip ahead to the next exercise.)

2. Look at your hand for fifteen seconds (wiggle fingers, flex open and close, make a peace sign). Write the name of someone who has the same number of hairs on each finger as you do.

3. Scribble ink on your thumb and make a thumbprint on a piece of paper. Go to the FBI and ask someone there to do a nationwide search for another person with your identical thumbprint. Write the name of this person.

4. Go into the bathroom, look closely in the mirror, and count the number of brown freckles on your nose (freckles only, no blackheads). Write the name of someone with the exact number of brown freckles.

5. Sneeze. Give the precise velocity, time span, and amount of nasal fluid expectorated from your nose and mouth. Write the name of someone who produces the exact amount.

6. Go to the dentist. Get an X ray of your teeth. Go back to the FBI and ask someone to do a Dental Records Search (DRS). Write the name of the person whose canines and bicuspids match yours.

7. (You'll need your friends to help you with this one.) Count the number of hairs on your head. If you lose count, you may want to start over by pulling them out, one at a time. Write the name of the person who has the same number of hairs as you.

8. Look in a mirror at the whites of your eyes. Count the number of bloodshot veins in both eyes. Write the name of the person who has the exact number of veins as you.

9. Write three extraordinary qualities you possess. Now write the name of the person who possesses the exact three qualities.

10. Read Psalm 139 and write the incredible things said about you. Then write the name of the person who wrote these great things about you.

You Gotta Do Right

(Living God's Way)

Right or wrong? Wrong or right? What about right and wrong? Can you have both? This life is filled with choices. What you choose is up to you, but what you choose also comes back to you. Jesus said you can tell a tree by its fruit. A good tree produces good fruit, and a bad tree makes rotten apples. What kind of fruit are you producing? If you want to produce good fruit, you gotta do right.

What you do, right or wrong, will affect how you feel about yourself. People who constantly do wrong are usually insecure, selfish, and unsure about who they really are. People who do right do so because they know why they're choosing to do right. In other words, it's easy to do wrong. Anyone can do it. It doesn't take much creativity or effort. But to do right takes a willful, deliberate choice.

Where is God when I want to live my life serving others, but I need a few ideas?
Wash yourselves, make yourselves clean; put away the evil of your doings from before My eyes. Cease to do evil, learn to do good; seek justice, rebuke the oppressor; defend the fatherless, plead for the widow (Isaiah 1:16–17).

Where is God when I have countless talks with a friend about the bad stuff he's doing, but he won't listen to me?
He who is unjust, let him be unjust still; he who is filthy, let him be filthy still; he who is righteous, let him be righteous still; he who is holy, let him be holy still (Revelation 22:11).

Where is God when I need help understanding how to do what's right? How can God's Word help me?
For the word of the LORD is right, and all His work is done in truth (Psalm 33:4)

Where is God when my friend doesn't believe that people sin?
For there is not a just man on earth who does good and does not sin (Ecclesiastes 7:20).

Where is God when I'm disillusioned because I hear my friends say they're Christians, but they act completely the opposite?
Little children, let no one deceive you. He who practices righteousness is righteous, just as He is righteous (1 John 3:7).

Where is God when I'm trying to figure out if I'm following God or not?
In this the children of God and the children of the devil are manifest: Whoever does not practice righteousness is not of God, nor is he who does not love his brother (1 John 3:10).

Where is God when I've realized that what I've been doing is wrong and I need His help to change?
Let us search out and examine our ways, and turn back to the LORD (Lamentations 3:40).

Where is God when I'm trying to change my attitude about people with no or low income?
He who oppresses the poor reproaches his Maker, but he who honors Him has mercy on the needy (Proverbs 14:31).

Where is God when I struggle with wanting to get other people's attention anytime I do something good?
Take heed that you do not do your charitable deeds before men, to be seen by them. Otherwise you have no reward from your Father in heaven (Matthew 6:1).

Where is God when I can't get over all the wrong things I've done in the past? Does God remember my past sins?
Then He adds, "Their sins and their lawless deeds I will remember no more" (Hebrews 10:17)

You're Thumbody

(Being Unique)

Do you ever feel like a thumb? Not connected like the rest. Or an oddball? Or maybe too unique? There are a lot of unique things in this world that people don't want to get close to: two-headed snakes, older men in Speedos, dogs foaming at the mouth. Scary, weird stuff.

If you feel uncomfortably unique, remember that you are a masterpiece in the making. You may feel like a detached appendage sometimes, but you make a difference to God. Being special to God is as real as your thumb being connected to your hand. The thumb is a critical part of the hand. Without it, you couldn't pick up spare change, grip ski poles, shake hands, or do thumb wars. You're unique. You're special. And there's no one in the whole world like you.

Where is God when my friends at youth group say I'm a good speaker, but my ego gets in the way?
But "he who glories, let him glory in the LORD" (2 Corinthians 10:17).

Where is God when I don't feel very talented and I wonder if God will help me discover what I can do?
If you then, being evil, know how to give good gifts to your children, how much more will your heavenly Father give the Holy Spirit to those who ask Him! (Luke 11:13).

Where is God when I've recently received a lot of money and I need a good example about how to give some of it away?
So He said, "Truly I say to you that this poor widow has put in more than all; for all these out of their abundance have put in offerings for God, but she out of her poverty put in all the livelihood that she had" (Luke 21:3–4).

Where is God when I want to know why He didn't give me the same gifts and abilities my friends have?
Having then gifts differing according to the grace that is given to us, let us use them: if prophecy, let us prophesy in proportion to our faith (Romans 12:6).

Where is God when I can't figure out my role in the church?
And God has appointed these in the church: first apostles, second prophets, third teachers, after that miracles, then gifts of healings, helps, administrations, varieties of tongues (1 Corinthians 12:28).

Where is God when my Christian friends have been talking about their "spiritual gifts"? I want to know what mine are.
Even so you, since you are zealous for spiritual gifts, let it be for the edification of the church that you seek to excel (1 Corinthians 14:12).

Where is God when I'm depressed because I feel like I have nothing to offer Him?
And whatever you ask in My name, that I will do, that the Father may be glorified in the Son. If you ask anything in My name, I will do it (John 14:13–14).

Where is God when I don't know how to ask Him to help me use my talents for His glory?
And in that day you will ask Me nothing. Most assuredly, I say to you, whatever you ask the Father in My name He will give you (John 16:23).

Chapter TWO

Why Me?

DON'T YOU LOVE it when bad things happen to people you don't like? What about the weird-looking guy in your math class who gets blamed for something he didn't do and everybody laughs at him? Or the sleazy girl who gets caught drinking at school? How about the jerk on the football team who gets kicked off the squad, and you suddenly get promoted from second-string to first-string? Isn't it great to see your enemies, the people who drive you nuts, being teased by classmates or suspended from school? Isn't it great when they learn the hard way that the world doesn't revolve around them?

Life is sweet when the sugar's in our bowl. But what about when things go sour, stale, or downright rotten for us? Then we whine, "Why me, God?" We think other people get what they deserve when bad things happen to them, but when bad things happen to us, we think life's unfair.

Life does throw some wild curveballs, and sometimes you're going to be standing too close to the plate and get hit. Eventually, we all get hit. That doesn't mean that God is the Nolan Ryan of the universe. He's not trying to peg us.

For reasons beyond explanation, God allows certain things to happen because He is God. He doesn't think like you or do things the way you would do things. His agenda is different from yours and mine. But when bad things happen to you, it doesn't mean that God doesn't love you. Far from it. God loves you unconditionally. Good and bad events are part of life. We learn about ourselves and our relationships with God and others by going through these events.

During any given day, you probably grumble at God plenty of times and wonder why He allows you to eat the raw end of the hot dog. You cannot know all of God's thoughts or reasons, but you can know His heart. You can know that He says He'll never leave or forsake you. You can know that nothing can separate you from His love. You can know that He's with you when everyone else has abandoned you. Why? Because Jesus knows what it's like to be abandoned. He knows what it's like to say "Why?" When Jesus was hanging on the cross, alone, with no one to help or comfort Him, He asked God why. "About the ninth hour Jesus cried out with a loud voice, saying, 'Eli, Eli, lama sabachthani?' that is, 'My God, My God, why have You forsaken me?'" (Matthew 27:46). Jesus knows why.

Did God Let Me Down?

(Disappointment)

Life is filled with disappointments. When things don't go as you planned or turn out as you thought, it's easy to feel like God let you down. God doesn't promise to take away problems. He does promise to be present in the midst of your problems.

When I'm frustrated or disappointed with God, it's usually because I'm frustrated with myself. Instead of running to Him for help, I tend to blame Him for my problems. Sound familiar? You and I will always let ourselves down, but God is always there to pick us up. He promises us His presence and His peace.

Where is God when I need to know that He'll never disappoint me?
Then you will know that I am the LORD, for they shall not be ashamed who wait for Me (Isaiah 49:23).

Where is God when I feel like it's hopeless putting my hope in Him?
Now hope does not disappoint, because the love of God has been poured out in our hearts by the Holy Spirit who was given to us (Romans 5:5).

Where is God when I'm afraid He won't help me out?
Have I not commanded you? Be strong and of good courage; do not be afraid, nor be dismayed, for the LORD your God is with you wherever you go (Joshua 1:9).

Where is God when I've had it easy, but now my life is really hard and I wonder if He has let me down?
Remember now, who ever perished being innocent? Or where were the upright ever cut off? Even as I have seen, those who plow iniquity and sow trouble reap the same (Job 4:7–8).

Where is God when I need His help?
Hear, O LORD, and have mercy on me; LORD, be my helper! You have turned for me my mourning into dancing; You have put off my sackcloth and clothed me with gladness (Psalm 30:10–11).

Where is God when I feel discouraged, even though I used to be a really strong Christian?
Therefore my spirit is overwhelmed within me; my heart within me is distressed. I remember the days of old; I meditate on all Your works; I muse on the work of Your hands (Psalm 143:4–5).

Where is God when I wonder if He is really reliable?
Therefore thus says the Lord GOD: "Behold, I lay in Zion a stone for a foundation, a tried stone, a precious cornerstone, a sure foundation; whoever believes will not act hastily" (Isaiah 28:16).

Where is God when I've prayed and prayed for Him to help me with temptation, but I'm still struggling?
No temptation has overtaken you except such as is common to man; but God is faithful, who will not allow you to be tempted beyond what you are able, but with the temptation will also make the way of escape, that you may be able to bear it (1 Corinthians 10:13).

Growing Beyond Bitterness

(Angry with God)

God's not very popular in this world. Many people are ticked off at Him. A lot of frustrated, enraged, bitter people blame Him for their unhappy families, world hunger, one-point losses, car crashes, failing grades, and ruthless teachers.

Growing beyond bitterness is impossible with a clenched fist. God opens His hand to you in friendship to walk with you every day of your life. Do you want to live a bitter life? How long can you stay angry with God? Bitterness leaves an awful taste in your soul. Pry open your fingers and accept God's friendship. What type of friend are you going to be?

Where is God when my heart has been hardened by bitterness?
I will give you a new heart and put a new spirit within you; I will take the heart of stone out of your flesh and give you a heart of flesh (Ezekiel 36:26).

Where is God when I need to be freed from past hurts and bitterness?
If you then, being evil, know how to give good gifts to your children, how much more will your Father who is in heaven give good things to those who ask Him! (Matthew 7:11).

Where is God when my heart easily gets bitter anytime others don't do what they promised?
Create in me a clean heart, O God, and renew a steadfast spirit within me (Psalm 51:10).

Where is God when I want to know if it's OK to tell Him how I really feel about my struggles?
Therefore I will not restrain my mouth; I will speak in the anguish of my spirit, I will complain in the bitterness of my soul (Job 7:11)

Where is God when I don't want to die an unhappy person? Can He help me be at peace with myself when I die?

One dies in his full strength, being wholly at ease and secure; His pails are full of milk, and the marrow of his bones is moist. Another man dies in the bitterness of his soul, never having eaten with pleasure (Job 21:23–25).

Where is God when I want to know what to do with my bitterness?

Let all bitterness, wrath, anger, clamor, and evil speaking be put away from you, with all malice (Ephesians 4:31).

Where is God when I get overwhelmed by bitterness and I don't know how to deal with it?

And she was in bitterness of soul, and prayed to the LORD and wept in anguish (1 Samuel 1:10).

Where is God when I feel like not following Him?

"Your own wickedness will correct you, and your backslidings will rebuke you. Know therefore and see that it is an evil and bitter thing that you have forsaken the LORD your God, and the fear of Me is not in you," says the Lord GOD of hosts (Jeremiah 2:19).

Where is God when I've got a friend who was hurt by other Christians and is really bitter about it?

Looking carefully lest anyone fall short of the grace of God; lest any root of bitterness springing up cause trouble, and by this many become defiled (Hebrews 12:15).

I Got a Raw Deal

(Attitudes)

Raw deals. Nobody orders them, but everybody gets them When you get a raw deal, you need to watch out for the poisonous bacteria that comes inside. Just like salmonella in chicken or makayupuke in sushi, raw deals can poison your attitude.

Bad attitudes equal bad living. Jesus Christ came to give us abundant life. Not a problem-free life, but security, peace, confidence, and hope through a relationship with Him. Raw deals don't have to produce bad attitudes. You can choose how to deal with your raw deal. You can let God carve your character into the image of Christ as He helps you grow closer to Him.

Where is God when my faith has been shaken by other Christians who were uncool to me?

Surely he will never be shaken; the righteous will be in everlasting remembrance (Psalm 112:6).

Where is God when someone blames me for stealing, but I haven't done anything?

The righteous is delivered from trouble, and it comes to the wicked instead (Proverbs 11:8).

Where is God when trying to be honest doesn't seem to be worth it?

As righteousness leads to life, so he who pursues evil pursues it to his own death (Proverbs 11:19).

Where is God when I'm always getting blamed for things I don't do?

For a righteous man may fall seven times and rise again, but the wicked shall fall by calamity (Proverbs 24:16).

Where is God when I'm sick of getting raw deals?

You have not yet resisted to bloodshed, striving against sin (Hebrews 12:4).

Where is God when all my problems seem meaningless?

If you endure chastening, God deals with you as with sons; for what son is there whom a father does not chasten? (Hebrews 12:7).

Where is God when I get picked on? Does Jesus understand what I'm feeling?

He was oppressed and He was afflicted, yet He opened not His mouth; He was led as a lamb to the slaughter, and as a sheep before its shearers is silent, so He opened not His mouth (Isaiah 53:7).

Where is God when no one understands my situation and I'll probably come out the loser?

For we do not have a High Priest who cannot sympathize with our weaknesses, but was in all points tempted as we are, yet without sin. Let us therefore come boldly to the throne of grace, that we may obtain mercy and find grace to help in time of need (Hebrews 4:15–16).

Where is God when I'm always overlooked for promotions at work? Does God notice me?

Behold, the eye of the LORD is on those who fear Him, on those who hope in His mercy (Psalm 33:18).

Helping Friends in Trouble

Helping friends in conflict is a delicate art. If you want to help a friend who's in trouble, but you're not exactly sure what to do, here are some important ideas about what helps and what hinders friendships:

- *Conflict.* Good friends help each other out during hard times. Wading through problems is possible with good friends. Nobody wants to walk through conflict alone. Conflict can make your friendships stronger.
- *Compassion.* Compassion means "shared pain." You're sharing the pain your friend feels. If you can be a compassionate friend, you'll have friends for life.
- *Confrontation.* Confrontation means getting in your friend's face and telling the truth. Many people want you to tell them what they want to hear. A true friend tells you what you need to hear.
- *Condoning.* When a friend blows it and you say, "Oh, that's OK," but you know it's not, you're condoning the behavior. Condoning is the opposite of taking a stand for what you believe to be true. It's letting a friend slide into a life-style that could be destructive. Condoning weakens friendships.

- *Condemnation.* Every friend hates this stuff. When you condemn a friend, you act as the judge, jury, and prosecutor. Good friends don't condemn one another. A struggling friend needs support, not condemnation. Your friend needs to know you are there to offer help and encouragement. Condemnation kills friendships.
- *Communication.* Communication solves problems. Becoming a good listener is the first step to effective communication. How many times have you solved your own problem just by talking it out to someone who cared enough to listen? You can be that person for your friend!

A Second Chance

(Living Beyond Regret)

The cost of making poor decisions is often guilt, regret, and ugly consequences. Looking back at what we should have done, would have done, or could have done is agonizing.

Fortunately, God is a God of second chances. And third chances. And fourth chances. In His goodness and forgiveness, He graciously gives us more chances than we deserve.

When you let others, yourself, or God down by making a bad decision, God gives you a second chance. But don't take it or God for granted. He loves you more than you can imagine. Just give your life to Him every day, and make your second chance work.

Where is God when I regret messing up our friendship?
For godly sorrow produces repentance leading to salvation, not to be regretted; but the sorrow of the world produces death (2 Corinthians 7:10).

Where is God when I feel like I'm still paying for something I did wrong a long time ago?

Sow for yourselves righteousness; reap in mercy; break up your fallow ground, for it is time to seek the LORD, till He comes and rains righteousness on you (Hosea 10:12).

Where is God when a friend tells me that you're doing something wrong only if you get caught?

Even as I have seen, those who plow iniquity and sow trouble reap the same (Job 4:8).

Where is God when I got forced into a fight? What can I do next time?

Now the fruit of righteousness is sown in peace by those who make peace (James 3:18).

Where is God when I feel guilty for not spending more time with Him? What can I do?

But this I say: He who sows sparingly will also reap sparingly, and he who sows bountifully will also reap bountifully (2 Corinthians 9:6).

Where is God when I regret thinking that my bad choices wouldn't affect my relationship with Him?

Do not be deceived, God is not mocked; for whatever a man sows, that he will also reap. For he who sows to his flesh will of the flesh reap corruption, but he who sows to the Spirit will of the Spirit reap everlasting life (Galatians 6:7–8).

Where is God when I wonder if I'm really any different from the way I was before I became a Christian?

Therefore, if anyone is in Christ, he is a new creation; old things have passed away; behold, all things have become new (2 Corinthians 5:17).

Where is God when I feel like I take Him for granted, knowing that He'll forgive me when I mess up?

What shall we say then? Shall we continue in sin that grace may abound? Certainly not! How shall we who died to sin live any longer in it? (Romans 6:1–2)

Where is God when I need to choose which path to follow in life?
Enter by the narrow gate; for wide is the gate and broad is the way that leads to destruction, and there are many who go in by it. Because narrow is the gate and difficult is the way which leads to life, and there are few who find it (Matthew 7:13–14).

Life's Not Fair

(Raw Deal #2)

I grew up with one brother and five sisters. I often felt like a pincushion for my sisters' fingernails. And I got blamed more than once for beating up my little brother when I never even touched him. Let's face it. Life's not fair.

Part of growing up is learning that life doesn't always operate on fairness. That doesn't mean life is never fair. That just means life won't always be fair. You can't force life to be fair.

The sooner you realize life is an adventure, the more you can enjoy the ride. When you're on an adventure, the unexpected always happens. Planes are missed, travel plans get messed up, luggage is lost, and the airplane food stinks. You can take the adventure as it comes and enjoy each day God gives you to live, or you can fold your arms, pout, and say, "This isn't fair."

If you do, you'll probably hear the same thing I often heard my parents say, "Tough."

Where is God when I'm trying to do what's right, but I see so much dishonesty?
He stores up sound wisdom for the upright; He is a shield to those who walk uprightly; He guards the paths of justice, and preserves the way of His saints (Proverbs 2:7–8).

Where is God when my youth pastor plays favorites?
For there is no partiality with God (Romans 2:11).

Where is God when I want to know how I can be fair with all my friends?
Then you will understand righteousness and justice, equity and every good path. When wisdom enters your heart, and knowledge is pleasant to your soul (Proverbs 2:9–10).

Where is God when I look at this world and wonder if He's really just?
What shall we say then? Is there unrighteousness with God? Certainly not! (Romans 9:14).

Where is God when it's not fair that others make fun of me for standing up for Him?
For this is commendable, if because of conscience toward God one endures grief, suffering wrongfully. For what credit is it if, when you are beaten for your faults, you take it patiently? But when you do good and suffer, if you take it patiently, this is commendable before God (1 Peter 2:19–20).

Where is God when it seems totally unfair that Jesus had to die for us? Why?
Who Himself bore our sins in His own body on the tree, that we, having died to sins, might live for righteousness—by whose stripes you were healed (1 Peter 2:24).

Where is God when it's not fair that I have so many struggles, but none of my friends do?
Many are the afflictions of the righteous, but the LORD delivers him out of them all (Psalm 34:19).

Where is God when it's not fair that my friend accused me of gossiping about her? What can I tell her to make her believe me?
The mouth of the righteous speaks wisdom, and his tongue talks of justice (Psalm 37:30).

Where is God when I want to know what qualities He wants me to show to others who have been unfair to me?

Unto the upright there arises light in the darkness; he is gracious, and full of compassion, and righteous (Psalm 112:4).

I Didn't Do It

(Getting Blamed)

When I was in seventh grade, I was wrongfully blamed for stealing money. I was at my friend's house, and his grandpa accused me of stealing seventy-five dollars from the kitchen counter. I didn't know what he was talking about. *I didn't steal his money. I didn't even see any money on the counter. Why is he blaming me?* I wondered.

He chased me out of the house and told me never to come back. He followed me into the front yard just as my dad was pulling into our driveway across the street. Seeing that something was going on, he got out of the car and crossed the street. "What's going on here, Joey?" he asked.

I burst into tears and pointed to the older man. "He says I stole his seventy-five dollars. I didn't take his money. I didn't do anything!"

"That boy isn't welcome in this house until he returns every penny of the money he took," the older man countered.

"Pipe down," my dad said to him. "He didn't take your money. He said he didn't and I believe him."

Thanks, Dad.

When you get nailed for something you didn't do, remember that God is your witness. He saw the whole thing. He'll stand up for you when no one else will. He trusts you when others accuse you.

I hope you have a dad on this earth as great as my dad. If not, your heavenly Dad is ready to tell your accusers, "Pipe down."

Where is God when I've been accused of not being a Christian because of some serious mistakes? What can I do to change?

Examine yourselves as to whether you are in the faith. Test yourselves. Do you not know yourselves, that Jesus Christ is in you?—unless indeed you are disqualified (2 Corinthians 13:5).

Where is God when I get in trouble for making poor decisions?
Test all things; hold fast what is good (1 Thessalonians 5:21).

Where is God when my best friend is mad at me for a fight she started?
Moreover if your brother sins against you, go and tell him his fault between you and him alone. If he hears you, you have gained your brother (Matthew 18:15).

Where is God when I get in trouble for arguing with my sister and I didn't even start it?
Do all things without complaining and disputing, that you may become blameless and harmless, children of God without fault in the midst of a crooked and perverse generation, among whom you shine as lights in the world (Philippians 2:14–15).

Where is God when I get blamed for being home late because I couldn't get a ride?
Therefore, to him who knows to do good and does not do it, to him it is sin (James 4:17).

Where is God when I always get blamed for doing something I didn't do?
Thus says the LORD of hosts, the God of Israel: "Amend your ways and your doings, and I will cause you to dwell in this place" (Jeremiah 7:3).

Where is God when the people I hang out with are always getting in trouble? A few of them say they're Christians, but God isn't top on their priority list.
They profess to know God, but in works they deny Him (Titus 1:16).

Where is God when my older brother gets all the attention because he never does anything wrong?

Not as Cain who was of the wicked one and murdered his brother. And why did he murder him? Because his works were evil and his brother's righteous (1 John 3:12).

Where is God when I get grounded for using foul language?
For we all stumble in many things. If anyone does not stumble in word, he is a perfect man, able also to bridle the whole body (James 3:2).

Poor Me

(Self-Pity)

Like Job, Dana suffered terrible hardships. Within four short years, Dana lost his father, lost the house he grew up in, and was diagnosed with cancer. His family belongings were burned in a house fire. He got shingles (large boils) all over his body. His 4 x 4 truck was stolen. He endured radiation, chemotherapy, and several major operations. He was ripped off by his insurance company, which was subsequently indicted for insurance fraud. If anyone had reason to curse God and whine, "Poor me," it was Dana.

While his health withered away, his smile and caring spirit breathed life. Never once did I hear Dana complain or curse his circumstances or his God.

Do I have much to complain about? I am humbled by Dana. He reminds me of Christ.

Where is God when I pout and complain when things don't go my way?
Only fear the LORD, and serve Him in truth with all your heart; for consider what great things He has done for you (1 Samuel 12:24).

Where is God when I'm depressed because I don't think He cares about my problems?

He will spare the poor and needy, and will save the souls of the needy (Psalm 72:13).

Where is God when I feel like I don't have any friends who support me?
For if they fall, one will lift up his companion. But woe to him who is alone when he falls, for he has no one to help him up (Ecclesiastes 4:10).

Where is God when my friend put a big dent in my car? I'm trying not to be too upset, but I really am.
Turn away my eyes from looking at worthless things, and revive me in Your way (Psalm 119:37).

Where is God when things don't happen as I expect? I seem to lose all hope in Him.
Are there any among the idols of the nations that can cause rain? Or can the heavens give showers? Are You not He, O LORD our God? Therefore we will wait for You, since You have made all these (Jeremiah 14:22).

Where is God when I'm sick of getting picked on by others?
I will call upon the LORD, who is worthy to be praised; so shall I be saved from my enemies (2 Samuel 22:4).

Where is God when my parents are making me apologize to our neighbors for toilet-papering their house?
Only let your conduct be worthy of the gospel of Christ (Philippians 1:27).

Where is God when people tell me that I need to grow up and stop complaining about my problems?
That you may walk worthy of the Lord, fully pleasing Him, being fruitful in every good work and increasing in the knowledge of God (Colossians 1:10).

Where is God when I don't understand what He's doing while I'm going through problems?

Every branch in Me that does not bear fruit He takes away; and every branch that bears fruit He prunes, that it may bear more fruit (John 15:2).

What Keeps Me Coming Back?

Why should you and I keep following Jesus Christ? With so much evil, suffering, hardship, doubt, and struggle in this world, why should we keep coming back to God every morning to say, "Not my will, but Your will be done"? Why keep asking God, "Why?" Out of all the choices we have, why take a road that is straight, narrow, confusing, challenging, and filled with obstacles? If you've made the decision to be the person God is creating you to be, what keeps you coming back to Him each day? Here's what keeps me coming back:

- *Allure.* Of all the mysteries in this world, none allures me more than the mystery of God. Wondering who God is, is a daily adventure. The apostle Paul said, "[I want to know Christ] and the power of His resurrection, and the fellowship of His sufferings, being conformed to His death" (Philippians 3:10). Following Christ is a search to know the God who intimately knows you and me.

- *Attraction.* Our refrigerator is covered with magnets holding up our favorite pictures of family and friends. I call it our Wall of Fame. Do you know that God has your picture on His refrigerator? Knowing that God passionately loves me draws me to Him every day. His love is attractive. It draws and connects me to Him stronger than any magnet on our fridge.

- *Awe.* I don't want to use an already overused word, so I'll just say God inspires me to be in awe of Him. (See, I didn't say awesome.) God creates a sense of wonder in me like nothing else in this world. Each morning, He paints the sky with a palette of colors. At dusk, He adds the final touches of red, pink, and orange. Deer run across my path as I ride my mountain bike through the hills. On a river's edge, two squealing otters wrestle and chase each other ten feet from where I sit. Five minutes later, a doe and her fawn come to drink from the cool water. My God is an awesome God. I don't care if that word is overused. It's true.

Allure. Attraction. Awe. These three things keep me coming back to God each day. What keeps you coming back?

Hey, God!

(Questioning God)

God can handle any question you throw at Him. Your questions can't intimidate, frighten, or startle Him. Your questions are important to God because He cares about you. He's not like a teacher who rolls his eyes when someone asks a question everyone else already knows the answer to. Each and every question you ask is meaningful to God.

Be careful about your attitude when asking God questions. Honest questions are worth answering. Some answers we discover sooner than others. When you've got a question on your mind, it's OK to shout, "Hey, God!" to get His attention. Just don't expect Him to stand at attention like a new recruit. He's God. He's got a bit more seniority than either of us.

Where is God when I feel like complaining about His way of doing things?
Woe to him who strives with his Maker! Let the potsherd strive with the potsherds of the earth! Shall the clay say to him who forms it, "What are you making?" Or shall your handiwork say, "He has no hands"? (Isaiah 45:9).

Where is God when I question His plans for my life?
The LORD brings the counsel of the nations to nothing; He makes the plans of the peoples of no effect. The counsel of the LORD stands

forever, the plans of His heart to all generations (Psalm 33:10–11).

Where is God when I want to give my plans to Him, but I'm afraid He won't guide me?
A man's heart plans his way, but the LORD directs his steps (Proverbs 16:9).

Where is God when I secretly think I can outsmart Him?
There is no wisdom or understanding or counsel against the LORD (Proverbs 21:30).

Where is God when I want to know if He understands my past and my future?
Declaring the end from the beginning, and from ancient times things that are not yet done, saying, "My counsel shall stand, and I will do all My pleasure" (Isaiah 46:10).

Where is God when I have a friend who thinks she can change His mind if she prays hard enough?
But He is unique, and who can make Him change? And whatever His soul desires, that He does (Job 23:13).

Where is God when I want to know who has ultimate control here on earth? God or human beings?
All the inhabitants of the earth are reputed as nothing; He does according to His will in the army of heaven and among the inhabitants of the earth. No one can restrain His hand or say to Him, "What have You done?" (Daniel 4:35).

Where is God when I wonder if He really created the earth?
I have made the earth, and created man on it. I—My hands—stretched out the heavens, and all their host I have commanded (Isaiah 45:12).

Where is God when I'm angry that He doesn't do what I want? Where is He?
But our God is in heaven; He does whatever He pleases (Psalm 115:3).

Who's to Blame?

(Taking Responsibility)

I didn't do it. Don't blame me. It's not my fault. It's easy to push off responsibility and avoid getting involved by blaming, pointing the finger, and expecting others to own up to problems that are really your own. Blaming others is a sign of immaturity.

God's Word tells us to look at our motives and actions. That includes accepting or avoiding responsibility. God knows when we blame others and when we own up. He knows if we're looking out for our own interests or the interests of others. Blaming others causes us to grow down. Accepting responsibility helps us grow up.

Where is God when I feel like backing out of a tough situation because I don't want to get blamed for something I didn't do?
Brethren, let each one remain with God in that state in which he was called (1 Corinthians 7:24).

Where is God when my friend says that I owe him money, but he owes me money? What can I do?
Owe no one anything except to love one another, for he who loves another has fulfilled the law (Romans 13:8).

Where is God when people in my youth group take advantage of each other?
Therefore you shall not oppress one another, but you shall fear your God; for I am the LORD your God (Leviticus 25:17).

Where is God when I wonder about His purpose in testing me?
And you shall remember that the LORD your God led you all the way these forty years in the wilderness, to humble you and test you, to know what was in your heart, whether you would keep His commandments or not (Deuteronomy 8:2).

Where is God when I need help being honest even when I might get in trouble?

I know also, my God, that You test the heart and have pleasure in uprightness (1 Chronicles 29:17).

Where is God when no one wants to take responsibility for the problems in our youth group?
But let each one examine his own work, and then he will have rejoicing in himself alone, and not in another (Galatians 6:4).

Where is God when my friend and I can't resolve our fight? How can God help us?
Let us search out and examine our ways, and turn back to the LORD (Lamentations 3:40).

Where is God when I wonder if it's OK to test Him?
Jesus said to him, "It is written again, 'You shall not tempt the Lord your God'" (Matthew 4:7).

Why Is There So Much Evil?

(Evil in the World)

Reading the front page of the newspaper is depressing. Today I read about starvation in Africa, strife in Bosnia/Herzegovina, car accidents, and neo-Nazi hate crimes in Germany. *Why is there so much evil in this world? Why does God allow it? If He's really in control, can't He do something?*

I've been thinking about these questions a lot lately, and I haven't discovered any easy answers. The only thing that makes sense to me is thinking about Jesus dying on a cross for the sins of humankind. I believe evil exists. I see it everywhere. I see it in other people and in myself. In the midst of a world slammed by natural disasters, human suffering, war, and broken families, Jesus is the only One who adequately addresses the problem of human suffering. Jesus confronted evil with His own flesh.

Evil has been sentenced to death. Evil won't be around much longer. I can hardly wait.

Where is God when I don't understand why so many educated people are atheists?
The wise men are ashamed, they are dismayed and taken. Behold, they have rejected the word of the LORD; so what wisdom do they have? (Jeremiah 8:9).

Where is God when I don't understand why evil people prosper and good people suffer?
I have seen everything in my days of vanity: There is a just man who perishes in his righteousness, and there is a wicked man who prolongs life in his wickedness (Ecclesiastes 7:15).

Where is God when it seems that wicked people never pay for their wickedness?
The righteousness of the blameless will direct his way aright, but the wicked will fall by his own wickedness (Proverbs 11:5).

Where is God when I can't understand why evil people keep being evil?
Let grace be shown to the wicked, yet he will not learn righteousness; in the land of uprightness he will deal unjustly, and will not behold the majesty of the LORD (Isaiah 26:10).

Where is God when I want to know how I'm supposed to make a difference for Him in an indifferent world?
You are the light of the world. A city that is set on a hill cannot be hidden. Nor do they light a lamp and put it under a basket, but on a lampstand, and it gives light to all who are in the house. Let your light so shine before men, that they may see your good works and glorify your Father in heaven (Matthew 5:14–16).

Where is God when Christians get persecuted for following Jesus?
But I say to you, love your enemies, bless those who curse you, do good to those who hate you, and pray for those who spitefully use you and persecute you (Matthew 5:44).

Where is God when it seems no one cares about doing what's right?

Woe to those who call evil good, and good evil; who put darkness for light, and light for darkness; who put bitter for sweet, and sweet for bitter! (Isaiah 5:20).

Where is God when so many people say they're Christians, but you can never tell?

Who is wise and understanding among you? Let him show by good conduct that his works are done in the meekness of wisdom (James 3:13).

Where is God when I want to know how to live in this world?

For you were once darkness, but now you are light in the Lord. Walk as children of light (Ephesians 5:8).

Where is God when I wonder if everyone has turned away from Him?

All we like sheep have gone astray; we have turned, every one, to his own way; and the LORD has laid on Him the iniquity of us all (Isaiah 53:6).

Chapter **THREE**

What God Says

EVER GET REJECTED by someone you really care about? I mean rejected with a capital R-E-J-E-C-T-E-D, slam dunk, in your face, you-are-not-worth-cereal-dust-left-at-the-bottom-of-the-box, get-out-of-my-face-out-of-my-way-out-of-my-life, can-I-spell-that-word-again—R-E-J-E-C-T-I-O-N! Ouch. Love has never been so lonely.

God knows what it's like to love someone and be rejected. He loves the whole, entire world, and He gets rejected all the time. How would you like it if you created something that could change the world and your idea got rejected? What if you created an ozone patch kit before the human race turns into raisins? What if you developed an Oxy-5,000,000 oil-slick degreaser that could clean the ocean? Or what if it was your idea behind the world's first non-polluting, trash-burning automobile engine? What if all these ideas and plans you created could radically redesign the way the world lives, but every single one of them was rejected? I think God would understand how you feel. He created the world and every person in it. He has a complete and perfect plan for every human being. But He still gets rejected by people all the time. No matter how good He is or how incredible His ideas are or how much He loves people, people still reject Him.

You'll understand that He always hangs out with you. If you've ever been rejected, you'll understand how He feels about rejection. Best of all, you'll learn that He will never reject you. That's what God says.

Creature Comforts

(God's Comfort)

Plush sofas. Soft pillows. A warm fire. Mellow music floating in the air. Complete relaxation. Aah . . . creature comforts. Living a life of ease and luxury is a fantasy most people dream about, but few experience.

For thousands of years, people in the midst of pain and hardship have gone daily to God's Word to find the comfort they need. God's Word is filled with thousands of promises to comfort and encourage you, no matter what you're facing. God, the God of all comfort, gives you the promise of His presence each and every day. He doesn't promise a life of luxury. He promises you His peace. No creature comfort could ever comfort you like that.

Where is God when I'm having an awful day?
Yea, though I walk through the valley of the shadow of death, I will fear no evil; for You are with me; Your rod and Your staff, they comfort me (Psalm 23:4).

Where is God when I wonder if He really comforts those who are suffering?
Nevertheless God, who comforts the downcast, comforted us by the coming of Titus (2 Corinthians 7:6).

Where is God when I need His word to comfort me?
I remembered Your judgments of old, O Lord, and have comforted myself (Psalm 119:52).

Where is God when I want to know if His love will comfort me anytime I need Him?
Let, I pray, Your merciful kindness be for my comfort, according to Your word to Your servant (Psalm 119:76).

Where is God when I made a bunch of serious mistakes because I was angry with Him, but I'm sorry for what I've done?

I have seen his ways, and will heal him; I will also lead him, and restore comforts to him and to his mourners (Isaiah 57:18).

Where is God when my heart is weighed down by all sorts of problems?
For I will turn their mourning to joy, will comfort them, and make them rejoice rather than sorrow (Jeremiah 31:13).

Where is God when others make fun of me for being a Christian?
Show me a sign for good, that those who hate me may see it and be ashamed, because You, LORD, have helped me and comforted me (Psalm 86:17).

Where is God when I'm depressed because my mom (dad) recently passed away?
Blessed are those who mourn, for they shall be comforted (Matthew 5:4).

Where is God when I want to praise Him for feeling His comfort through a difficult problem?
Sing, O heavens! Be joyful, O earth! And break out in singing, O mountains! For the LORD has comforted His people, and will have mercy on His afflicted (Isaiah 49:13).

Church Chat

(God's People)

The church is God's people. The church isn't a funky old building or a glass skyscraper reaching to the heavens. The church is a community of people. And people are weird. That means there are going to be weird people in church. God's weird church. The church He loves.

A lot of people stay out of church because they think they have to be perfect or have their lives all together to attend. No way. Even though some people talk about others being the pillars of the church and strong Christians, the only "strong" Christians are those who recognize their weaknesses. Weak Christians give control of their lives to God. If you've stayed away from church because of weird people or because you think you're not good enough to go, don't worry. You're invited. There's plenty of room in God's weird and weak church. The one He loves.

Where is God when my youth pastor bugs me to show up? What can I tell him?

For though I am absent in the flesh, yet I am with you in spirit, rejoicing to see your good order and the steadfastness of your faith in Christ (Colossians 2:5).

Where is God when I hear that just going to church won't get me to heaven?

That if you confess with your mouth the Lord Jesus and believe in your heart that God has raised Him from the dead, you will be saved. For with the heart one believes unto righteousness, and with the mouth confession is made unto salvation (Romans 10:9–10).

Where is God when the people at my church seem to be complete hypocrites?

How can you say to your brother, "Brother, let me remove the speck that is in your eye," when you yourself do not see the plank that is in your own eye? Hypocrite! First remove the plank from your own eye, and then you will see clearly to remove the speck that is in your brother's eye (Luke 6:42).

Where is God when my youth director is a total geek, but the church down the street has a cool one?

God Himself is with us as our head (2 Chronicles 13:12).

Where is God when my parents won't let me go on an inner-city mission trip with all my friends?

Praying always with all prayer and supplication in the Spirit, being watchful to this end with all perseverance and supplication for all the saints (Ephesians 6:18).

Where is God when my youth group is interested only in numbers and no one's interested in me?
O LORD, You know; remember me and visit me (Jeremiah 15:15).

Where is God when my church doesn't try to make Christianity relevant to my life?
And now, Israel, what does the LORD your God require of you, but to fear the LORD your God, to walk in all His ways and to love Him, to serve the LORD your God with all your heart and with all your soul, and to keep the commandments of the LORD and His statutes which I command you today for your good? (Deuteronomy 10:12–13).

Where is God when my church is totally B-O-R-I-N-G?
They all slumbered and slept (Matthew 25:5).

Where is God when I can't understand why some religious people are so phony?
Pure and undefiled religion before God and the Father is this: to visit orphans and widows in their trouble, and to keep oneself unspotted from the world (James 1:27).

Where is God when I've had a very negative experience with church? What should I do?
Beware, brethren, lest there be in any of you an evil heart of unbelief in departing from the living God; but exhort one another daily, while it is called "Today," lest any of you be hardened through the deceitfulness of sin (Hebrews 3:12–13).

Where is God when I can't stand weird Christians?
For who makes you differ from another? (1 Corinthians 4:7).

Erasing the Board

(Forgiveness)

I was never good at math. All the numbers, equations, formulas, and theoretic postulations never made sense to me. I hated being called to the board to solve problems. As I walked to the board, I could smell chalk dust and my own fear. Addition wasn't a problem, but geometry had my head spinning in bisecting trapezoids. Math reminded me of my mistakes. My favorite part of standing at the chalkboard was grabbing the eraser and wiping away my incorrect answer. My mistakes wiped into eternity.

How many millions of times has your math teacher erased the chalkboard? Can your English teachers remember all their students' grammatical blunders they've corrected? Can you remember every single mistake you've made on every test you've taken?

We tend to forget the things we hate. God is the same way. He forgets about the one thing He hates most: sin. When you ask for forgiveness after making a mistake, God erases your sin through His Son, Jesus Christ. He hates sin so much that He'll wipe it away as soon as you ask Him. That's how much He loves you. He chucks your sin as far as east is from west. (Try measuring that one!)

Where is God when I want to know what Jesus' forgiveness is all about?
In Him we have redemption through His blood, the forgiveness of sins, according to the riches of His grace (Ephesians 1:7).

Where is God when I doubt that He wants to forgive my sins?
I will cleanse them from all their iniquity by which they have sinned against Me (Jeremiah 33:8).

Where is God when I want to know if I'm supposed to forgive others just as God forgives me?
For if you forgive men their trespasses, your heavenly Father will also forgive you. But if you do not forgive men their trespasses, neither will your Father forgive your trespasses (Matthew 6:14–15).

Where is God when I want to know if He remembers my sins?
For I will be merciful to their unrighteousness, and their sins and their lawless deeds I will remember no more (Hebrews 8:12).

Where is God when I'm afraid to ask Him for forgiveness?
If we confess our sins, He is faithful and just to forgive us our sins and to cleanse us from all unrighteousness (1 John 1:9).

Where is God when I feel like hiding my sin, but I know I shouldn't?
I acknowledged my sin to You, and my iniquity I have not hidden. I said, "I will confess my transgressions to the LORD," and You forgave the iniquity of my sin. (Psalm 32:5).

Where is God when I'm so frustrated by committing the same sin over and over again?
Iniquities prevail against me; as for our transgressions, You will provide atonement for them (Psalm 65:3).

Where is God when I wonder if He forgives all my sins or just a few?
You have forgiven the iniquity of Your people; You have covered all their sin. (Psalm 85:2).

Where is God when I don't want to take His forgiveness for granted?
And you, being dead in your trespasses and the uncircumcision of your flesh, He has made alive together with Him, having forgiven you all trespasses (Colossians 2:13).

Eternity Matters

(Life and Death)

I grew up with death. Ever since I was a little kid, I've been surrounded by death. My dad is a mortician. An undertaker. He buries people for a living and helps grieving families. Try explaining that one during Show and Tell.

Have you ever considered how long eternity is? Life on earth is short. There's a big gap between life on earth and eternity. Eternity matters. If I knew I was going somewhere for longer than the average vacation time, I'd want to be prepared. Well prepared.

The Bible has loads to say about life after death. Jesus Christ came to earth so we could spend eternity with His Father. The Bible says God has put eternity in the hearts of people (Ecclesiastes 3:11), and without a personal relationship with Him, we will be forever separated from Him. That's a long time. In Christ Jesus, God promises that eternity is worth getting prepared for. Not preparing for eternity is wasted living.

Where is God when I want to be sure that Jesus is the way to get to heaven?

Jesus said to him, "I am the way, the truth, and the life. No one comes to the Father except through Me" (John 14:6).

Where is God when I want to know what eternal life is all about?

Most assuredly, I say to you, he who hears My word and believes in Him who sent Me has everlasting life, and shall not come into judgment, but has passed from death into life (John 5:24).

Where is God when I'm scared that there's nothing after this life and death is final?

"O Death, where is your sting? O Hades, where is your victory?" The sting of death is sin, and the strength of sin is the law. But thanks be to God, who gives us the victory through our Lord Jesus Christ (1 Corinthians 15:55–57).

Where is God when I want to be sure that He will welcome me into heaven?

I go to prepare a place for you. And if I go and prepare a place for you, I will come again and receive you to Myself; that where I am, there you may be also (John 14:2–3).

Where is God when I'm not sure if He has me included in His plans for heaven?

For I know the thoughts that I think toward you, says the LORD, thoughts of peace and not of evil, to give you a future and a hope (Jeremiah 29:11).

Where is God when I wonder what heaven will be like?

Behold, the tabernacle of God is with men, and He will dwell with them, and they shall be His people. God Himself will be with them and be their God. And God will wipe away every tear from their eyes; there shall be no more death, nor sorrow, nor crying. There shall be no more pain, for the former things have passed away (Revelation 21:3-4).

Where is God when I want to know if it's important to believe in Christ's resurrection?

But if there is no resurrection of the dead, then Christ is not risen. And if Christ is not risen, then our preaching is empty and your faith is also empty (1 Corinthians 15:13-14).

Where is God when I wonder if He wants everyone to have a relationship with Jesus Christ?

And this is the will of Him who sent Me, that everyone who sees the Son and believes in Him may have everlasting life; and I will raise him up at the last day (John 6:40).

Where is God when I want to know if eternal life is found in Jesus Christ?

And we know that the Son of God has come and has given us an understanding, that we may know Him who is true; and we are in Him who is true, in His Son Jesus Christ. This is the true God and eternal life (1 John 5:20).

Faithful Friend

(Counting on Jesus)

What friend of yours will hang on every word you speak and never cut in with poor advice? What friend of yours isn't a flake?

What friend of yours can you count on all the time, no matter what? What friend of yours is completely trustworthy? Will never gossip about you? Believes in you even when you don't believe in yourself? Makes you laugh when you feel like crying? Hangs out with you whenever you want? Likes the things that you like? Picks you first when choosing teams? Calls you every day? Loves you for who you are and not for the dumb things you do? Writes you love letters? Wakes you with the morning sun? Closes your day with a beautiful sunset? Flings stars in the heavens to sparkle in your eyes? Applauds for you louder than anyone else? Paints rainbows to remind you of a promise? Creates mountains for you to climb? Creates oceans and rivers for you to swim in? Is faithful to you even when you're not? Loves you more than anybody could or ever will? Would trade His life for yours? Have you ever had such a faithful friend as Jesus?

Where is God when I want to know if He's faithful even when I'm not?
If we are faithless, He remains faithful; He cannot deny Himself (2 Timothy 2:13).

Where is God when I break commitments? Does God break His commitments?
He is the Rock, His work is perfect; for all His ways are justice, a God of truth and without injustice; righteous and upright is He (Deuteronomy 32:4).

Where is God when I want to know if I'm faithful to Him, will He be faithful to me?
With the merciful You will show Yourself merciful; with a blameless man You will show Yourself blameless (2 Samuel 22:26).

Where is God when I need to know that He is faithful in everything He does?
For the word of the LORD is right, and all His work is done in truth (Psalm 33:4).

Where is God when I need to know that He'll help me get out of tempting situations?
No temptation has overtaken you except such as is common to man; but God is faithful, who will not allow you to be tempted beyond what you are able, but with the temptation will also make the way of escape, that you may be able to bear it (1 Corinthians 10:13).

Where is God when I want to know if He'll keep me walking with Him?
Now may the God of peace Himself sanctify you completely; and may your whole spirit, soul, and body be preserved blameless at the coming of our Lord Jesus Christ. He who calls you is faithful, who also will do it (1 Thessalonians 5:23–24).

Where is God when I want to know how faithful a friend He is?
Your mercy, O LORD, is in the heavens; Your faithfulness reaches to the clouds (Psalm 36:5).

Where is God when I've heard that He's faithful, but is that all?
But You, O Lord, are a God full of compassion, and gracious, longsuffering and abundant in mercy and truth (Psalm 86:15).

Where is God when I want to know if He's faithful to protect me from harm?
But the Lord is faithful, who will establish you and guard you from the evil one (2 Thessalonians 3:3).

Solo with God

Do you still have a favorite playground? I do. My favorite place to play is Joshua Tree National Monument. It has such an unbelievable amount of rocks; it's as if God grabbed Mount Everest, crumbled it into bits, and threw it over the high desert. The monument is popular for rich blue skies, golden sunsets, wildflowers, and the very spiny, spindly Joshua tree. (WARNING: Never sit on a Joshua tree!)

J.T. is the place where I like to challenge teenagers to do two things: (1) rock climb with ropes, harnesses, and equipment, and (2) be solo with God. The first challenge deals with acrophobia, the fear of heights. We put about sixty feet of air between the student and the ground, and we assure each person that it's the landing, not the fall, that hurts. As scary as the first challenge sounds, rock climbing is like walking on the sidewalk compared to the second challenge, which deals with alone-a-phobia, fear of going solo. Each student is challenged to be by himself or herself for at least an hour. Maybe two. No friends. No Walkman. No TV. No noise. Just the student, God, and the rocks.

A solo is a one-on-one time for you and God. You may be by yourself, but you're not alone. You're with your Creator. Most students, even most adults, know very little about what it means to be alone with God. Solo gives you a chance to learn about three significant things:

- *Solitude.* Being by yourself makes you look at who you really are. Scary thought! God wants to meet you during these alone times to give you His grace to face your weaknesses through His strength.
- *Silence.* God created the world in silence. We tend to live very noisy lives. Silence helps you hear God's voice by quieting all the other distractions in your life. God whispers louder than He shouts.
- *Surrender.* Sitting back in a harness over a one-hundred-foot cliff is a whole lot easier than saying each day, "OK, God, I surrender. I give up. You're in control now. I trust You with my life." Total surrender is roping up with God, knowing that climbing without a rope is for fools and dead people.

Before Jesus started His public ministry, He went into the desert for a forty-day solo. You and I will probably never spend forty days alone with God in the desert as Jesus did. (How would you explain that one to the attendance office?) But you can start today by having a solo time with your Creator wherever you are. He's crazy about spending time with you. A few minutes. Half an hour. A few hours. Solitude. Silence. Surrender. Solo helps get your life in order. Solo double-checks to make sure you've got your rope on tight. Solo gets you climbing with God.

God Is Love

(God's Love)

You've seen them on walls, bumper stickers, tattoos, freeway overpasses, T-shirts, "Monday Night Football," jewelry, billboards, and notebooks. The words *God is love* show up all over the place.

People are trying to get the message out any way they can. They have gone to extremes to spread the good news of Jesus Christ. Maybe they've gone too extreme.

The most effective way to tell others about God's unconditional love is to write it on your heart. If His love is in your heart, others can't miss it.

Where is God when I want to know what love is?
In this is love, not that we loved God, but that He loved us and sent His Son to be the propitiation for our sins (1 John 4:10).

Where is God when I want to know if He will always love me even when I fail to love Him?
And I said: "I pray, LORD God of heaven, O great and awesome God, You who keep Your covenant and mercy with those who love You and observe Your commandments" (Nehemiah 1:5).

Where is God when I want to think about how much He loves me?
We have thought, O God, on Your lovingkindness, in the midst of Your temple (Psalm 48:9).

Where is God when I need to experience His unconditional love and forgiveness?

Have mercy upon me, O God, according to Your lovingkindness; according to the multitude of Your tender mercies, blot out my transgressions (Psalm 51:1).

Where is God when I wonder if He ever holds back His love for me?

Blessed be God, who has not turned away my prayer, nor His mercy from me! (Psalm 66:20).

Where is God when I need His love to calm me down?

The LORD your God in your midst, the Mighty One, will save; He will rejoice over you with gladness, He will quiet you with His love, He will rejoice over you with singing (Zephaniah 3:17).

Where is God when I want to know how He proved His love for me?

But God demonstrates His own love toward us, in that while we were still sinners, Christ died for us (Romans 5:8).

Where is God when I want to tell my friend how God shows His love to us?

In this the love of God was manifested toward us, that God has sent His only begotten Son into the world, that we might live through Him (1 John 4:9).

Where is God when I feel empty and I need to be assured of His love?

But whoever keeps His word, truly the love of God is perfected in him. By this we know that we are in Him (1 John 2:5).

Where is God when I wonder if anything can separate me from His love?

Who shall separate us from the love of Christ? Shall tribulation, or distress, or persecution, or famine, or nakedness, or peril, or sword? . . . I am persuaded that neither death nor life, nor angels nor principalities nor powers, nor things present nor things to come, nor height nor depth, nor any other created thing, shall be able to separate us from the love of God which is in Christ Jesus our Lord (Romans 8:35, 38–39).

Where is God when I'm eager to know more about His love for me?
Therefore know that the LORD your God, He is God, the faithful God who keeps covenant and mercy for a thousand generations with those who love Him and keep His commandments (Deuteronomy 7:9).

Where is God when I need to remember what His love is all about?
But You are God, ready to pardon, gracious and merciful, slow to anger, abundant in kindness (Nehemiah 9:17).

God's Blueprint

(God's Word)

I called my friend Ted the other day and asked him what he was doing. "Oh, just spending some time in the blueprint," he replied. Ted is studying architecture, but I knew he wasn't in the middle of a project, so I asked, "Blueprint? What are you talking about?" I should have guessed. Ted said, "The Bible. I'm studying the blueprint for life." Duh.

Just like Ted, God is into architecture and design. Ted is good at what he does, but God is a lot better. His Word is the complete blueprint you need for your life. God is the master architect, and He has an original design for your life. How much do these plans cost? God's plan for your life is absolutely free. The only thing you need to use God's blueprint is a personal relationship with Christ.

Where is God when I want to know more about the Bible, but I get so confused?
Teach me Your way, O LORD; I will walk in Your truth; unite my heart to fear Your name (Psalm 86:11).

Where is God when I want His Word to be in my heart?

I delight to do Your will, O my God, and Your law is within my heart (Psalm 40:8).

Where is God when I often wonder what the Bible can do in my life?
For the word of God is living and powerful, and sharper than any two-edged sword, piercing even to the division of soul and spirit, and of joints and marrow, and is a discerner of the thoughts and intents of the heart (Hebrews 4:12).

Where is God when I doubt if everything the Bible says is true?
For thus says the LORD, who created the heavens, who is God, who formed the earth and made it, who has established it, who did not create it in vain, who formed it to be inhabited: "I am the LORD, and there is no other. I have not spoken in secret, in a dark place of the earth; I did not say to the seed of Jacob, 'Seek Me in vain'; I, the LORD, speak righteousness, I declare things that are right" (Isaiah 45:18–19).

Where is God when I get bored reading the Bible and I need to see things in a fresh perspective?
Open my eyes, that I may see wondrous things from Your law (Psalm 119:18).

Where is God when I wonder if His Word is relevant to every area of my life?
Every word of God is pure; He is a shield to those who put their trust in Him (Proverbs 30:5).

Where is God when I try reading the Bible, but I need someone to teach me more?
Show me Your ways, O LORD; teach me Your paths (Psalm 25:4).

Where is God when I'm eager to learn more about the Bible, but I don't know where to start?
If you cry out for discernment, and lift up your voice for understanding, if you seek her as silver, and search for her as for hidden treasures; then you will understand the fear of the LORD, and find the knowledge of God (Proverbs 2:3–5).

Where is God when I know I should read my Bible more, but I always seem to lack desire?
Yes, in the way of Your judgments, O LORD, we have waited for You; the desire of our soul is for Your name and for the remembrance of You (Isaiah 26:8).

Where is God when I make mistakes because I don't always know what's right or wrong? Will His Word teach me the difference?
Teach me, O LORD, the way of Your statutes, and I shall keep it to the end (Psalm 119:33).

Good Enough

(God's Goodness)

Raising a two-year-old to be a good little girl is a fun, yet chaotic, adventure. Janae is a creative, curious bundle of energy with a personality that's tough to harness. One of her passions is exploring and playing with anything that can cause bodily harm. *Janae, put down that knife. Janae, get away from the light socket. Janae, take the keys out of the ignition.*

Life with Janae is never dull. Her curiosity propels her into every day with enthusiasm and wonder. Sometimes, though, she wants to be the captain of her own ship, setting her own course with her three favorite words: *no, why,* and *mine.* When she begins to act out her own version of *Mutiny on the Bounty,* my wife and I look at each other and say, "I think she needs a time-out." Janae is a good little girl, most of the time. But sometimes she needs a little extra teaching.

You, Janae, and I have to learn about goodness through the magnifying lens of our mistakes. We're all like little kids discovering God's goodness. In Christ, we're learning to be good. Not on our own power, but on His. That's good.

Where is God when I want to thank Him for all His goodness to me?
Praise the LORD! Oh, give thanks to the LORD, for He is good! For His mercy endures forever (Psalm 106:1).

Where is God when I need confidence that His goodness will carry me through my struggles?
I would have lost heart, unless I had believed that I would see the goodness of the LORD in the land of the living (Psalm 27:13).

Where is God when I wonder if I'll experience His goodness by trusting in Him?
Oh, how great is Your goodness, which You have laid up for those who fear You, which You have prepared for those who trust in You in the presence of the sons of men! (Psalm 31:19).

Where is God when I'm skeptical about how good He is?
Then He said, "I will make all My goodness pass before you, and I will proclaim the name of the LORD before you" (Exodus 33:19).

Where is God when I wonder if His goodness will always be with me?
Surely goodness and mercy shall follow me all the days of my life; and I will dwell in the house of the LORD forever (Psalm 23:6).

Where is God when I need Him to answer my prayers?
Hear me, O LORD, for Your lovingkindness is good; turn to me according to the multitude of Your tender mercies (Psalm 69:16).

Where is God when I need His goodness to keep me going as a Christian?
He who has begun a good work in you will complete it until the day of Jesus Christ (Philippians 1:6).

Where is God when I'm amazed at how much He has blessed my life?
What shall I render to the LORD for all His benefits toward me? (Psalm 116:12).

His Story

Was He just a historical figure like Michelangelo? Was He some sort of magician? Did He really do miracles like people say He did? Is this guy Jesus for real? Who does He say He is? Who does the Bible say He is?

Jesus existed yesterday, and He exists today and *mañana*. A friend of mine told me, "The Bible, God's love letter to you, is *His-story: the story of Jesus*." Here are just a few verses that will tell you who Jesus is. Make history. Make Jesus the center of your life story.

Jesus is the First and the Last, the Beginning and the End.

I am the Alpha and the Omega, the Beginning and the End, the First and the Last (Revelation 22:13).

Jesus is the Son of God.

Then they all said, "Are You then the Son of God?" So He said to them, "You rightly say that I am" (Luke 22:70).

Jesus is the Son of Man.

But He kept silent and answered nothing. Again the high priest asked Him, saying to Him, "Are You the Christ, the Son of the Blessed?" Jesus said, "I am. And you will see the Son of Man sitting at the right hand of the Power, and coming with the clouds of heaven" (Mark 14:61–62).

Jesus is the Messiah.

The woman said to Him, "I know that Messiah is coming" (who is called Christ). "When He comes, He will tell us all things." Jesus said to her, "I who speak to you am He" (John 4:25–26).

Jesus is the Christ.

He said to them, "But who do you say that I am?" Peter answered and said to Him, "You are the Christ" (Mark 8:29).

Jesus is the Holy One of God.

Let us alone! What have we to do with You, Jesus of Nazareth?

Did You come to destroy us? I know who You are—the Holy One of God! (Luke 4:34).

Jesus is the Word of God.

And the Word became flesh and dwelt among us, and we beheld His glory, the glory as of the only begotten of the Father, full of grace and truth (John 1:14).

Jesus is the Lamb of God.

The next day John saw Jesus coming toward him, and said, "Behold! The Lamb of God who takes away the sin of the world!" (John 1:29).

Jesus is the Lord.

That if you confess with your mouth the Lord Jesus and believe in your heart that God has raised Him from the dead, you will be saved (Romans 10:9).

Jesus is our Savior.

For there is born to you this day in the city of David a Savior, who is Christ the Lord (Luke 2:11).

Jesus is our Teacher.

You call me Teacher and Lord, and you say well, for so I am (John 13:13).

Jesus is the Root and the Offspring of David, the Bright and Morning Star.

I, Jesus, have sent My angel to testify to you these things in the churches. I am the Root and the Offspring of David, the Bright and Morning Star (Revelation 22:16).

He is the true God and eternal life.

We know that the Son of God has come and has given us an understanding, that we may know Him who is true; and we are in Him who is true, in His Son Jesus Christ. This is the true God and eternal life (1 John 5:20).

Jesus is the way, the truth, and the life.

Jesus said to him, "I am the way, the truth, and the life. No one comes to the Father except through Me" (John 14:6).

Jesus is the true vine.

I am the true vine, and My Father is the vinedresser (John 15:1).

Jesus is the light of the world.

As long as I am in the world, I am the light of the world (John 9:5).

Jesus is the good shepherd.

I am the good shepherd; and I know My sheep, and am known by My own (John 10:14).

Jesus is the door for His sheep.

Then Jesus said to them again, "Most assuredly, I say to you, I am the door of the sheep" (John 10:7).

Jesus is the resurrection and the life.

Jesus said to her, "I am the resurrection and the life. He who believes in Me, though he may die, he shall live" (John 11:25).

Jesus is our great High Priest.

Seeing then that we have a great High Priest who has passed through the heavens, Jesus the Son of God, let us hold fast our confession (Hebrews 4:14).

Jesus is the bread of life.

And Jesus said to them, "I am the bread of life. He who comes to Me shall never hunger, and he who believes in Me shall never thirst" (John 6:35).

Jesus is not of "this world."

And He said to them, "You are from beneath; I am from above. You are of this world; I am not of this world" (John 8:23).

Jesus is gentle.

Take My yoke upon you and learn from Me, for I am gentle and lowly in heart, and you will find rest for your souls (Matthew 11:29).

Jesus is the righteous One.

My little children, these things I write to you, so that you may not sin. And if anyone sins, we have an Advocate with the Father, Jesus Christ the righteous (1 John 2:1).

Jesus is the great "I AM" (that means, past, present, and future—He's always existed).

Jesus said to them, "Most assuredly, I say to you, before Abraham was, I AM" (John 8:58).

Jesus is the Almighty.

"I am the Alpha and the Omega, the Beginning and the End," says the Lord, "who is and who was and who is to come, the Almighty" (Revelation 1:8).

Jesus is the living One.

I am He who lives, and was dead, and behold, I am alive forevermore. Amen. And I have the keys of Hades and of Death (Revelation 1:18).

Jesus is the One who searches minds and hearts.

I will kill her children with death, and all the churches shall know that I am He who searches the minds and hearts. And I will give to each one of you according to your works (Revelation 2:23).

Jesus never changes.

Jesus Christ is the same yesterday, today, and forever (Hebrews 13:8).

Jesus is coming soon.

He who testifies to these things says, "Surely I am coming quickly." Amen. Even so, come, Lord Jesus! (Revelation 22:20).

Side By Side

(God's Presence)

When I was a junior in college, I studied in Spain for three months. I learned some *español,* and I also got a quick education in the art of being robbed at knife point. Sitting in a park one Saturday afternoon, I was writing postcards home. Out of the corner of my eye, I saw two guys approaching me, and before I knew it, they were sitting at my side holding two long blood-producing knives. One at my heart. The other at my gut. They scrounged through my knapsack, took my watch (imitation Casio), and riffled through my wallet, which had only a dollar in it. *(No dinero, hombres . . . Olé!)*

I was praying, praying hard and fast: *Lord, please, please, please, don't let them stick those things in me! Please, God, please, please, please!* In the midst of getting my wits scared out of me, a sudden peace zoomed through me. Whoosh! I really felt the presence of Christ with me. Side by side.

You don't have to get held up to know that Jesus is always with you. He promises to never leave your side. He is always with you. Side by side.

Where is God when I want to tell others about His presence in my life?
But it is good for me to draw near to God; I have put my trust in the Lord GOD, that I may declare all Your works (Psalm 73:28).

Where is God when it seems that I'm the only Christian at my school?
Fear not, for I am with you; be not dismayed, for I am your God (Isaiah 41:10).

Where is God when I wonder if Jesus is with me anytime I feel alone in the midst of a crowd?
And lo, I am with you always, even to the end of the age (Matthew 28:20).

Where is God when my relationship with Him never seems to go anywhere?

So that He may establish your hearts blameless in holiness before our God and Father at the coming of our Lord Jesus Christ with all His saints (1 Thessalonians 3:13).

Where is God when I wonder if He really hears my prayers?

For what great nation is there that has God so near to it, as the LORD our God is to us, for whatever reason we may call upon Him? (Deuteronomy 4:7).

Where is God when I wonder if someone as insignificant as I am can ever get close to Him?

Even the sparrow has found a home, and the swallow a nest for herself, where she may lay her young—even Your altars, O LORD of hosts, my King and my God (Psalm 84:3).

Where is God when I feel guilty after ignoring Him for so long?

Let us draw near with a true heart in full assurance of faith, having our hearts sprinkled from an evil conscience and our bodies washed with pure water (Hebrews 10:22).

Where is God when I have to move away from all my Christian friends?

I am with you and will keep you wherever you go (Genesis 28:15).

Where is God when my parents are changing churches and I'm concerned that the people in the youth group may not be friendly to a newcomer?

"Do not be afraid of their faces, for I am with you to deliver you," says the LORD (Jeremiah 1:8).

Where is God when I don't feel His presence in my life?

And the LORD, He is the One who goes before you. He will be with you, He will not leave you nor forsake you; do not fear nor be dismayed (Deuteronomy 31:8).

Talking to God

(Persisting in Prayer)

Writing a book takes a long time. Writing a book takes even longer if you're trying to look up 1,001 Bible verses. My friend Jake is a sophomore in high school and a climbing fanatic. He calls me at least two or three times a week to go climbing. For the past two months, I've turned him down: "Sorry, Jake, I've got to write." Every time I see him at church he says the same thing, "When are we going climbing? Have you finished that stupid book yet?" What I like about Jake is that he's persistent. He never gives up. That's what it takes to become a good climber. Persistence is also what it takes to talk to God.

Most of us are really good at asking God for things but not very good at seeking and knocking. Persistence is nonstop seeking and knocking. Be persistent. Keep seeking. Keep knocking. Keep talking to God. Be like Jake. Keep calling.

Where is God when I wonder if He really hears my prayers?
The LORD is far from the wicked, but He hears the prayer of the righteous (Proverbs 15:29).

Where is God when I feel guilty asking Him to help me?
The LORD is good, a stronghold in the day of trouble; and He knows those who trust in Him (Nahum 1:7).

Where is God when I want to know how Jesus taught His disciples to pray?
In this manner, therefore, pray: Our Father in heaven, hallowed be Your name. Your kingdom come. Your will be done on earth as it is in heaven. Give us this day our daily bread. And forgive us our debts, as we forgive our debtors. And do not lead us into temptation, but deliver us from the evil one (Matthew 6:9–13).

Where is God when I wonder what the Bible says about the power of prayer?

The effective. fervent prayer of a righteous man avails much (James 5:16).

Where is God when I fall asleep during my prayer time?
Watch and pray, lest you enter into temptation. The spirit indeed is willing, but the flesh is weak (Mark 14:38).

Where is God when I'm praying a lot or not at all? How can I be more consistent?
Rejoicing in hope, patient in tribulation, continuing steadfastly in prayer (Romans 12:12).

Where is God when I feel like I'm talking to myself as I pray?
The sacrifice of the wicked is an abomination to the LORD, but the prayer of the upright is His delight (Proverbs 15:8).

Where is God when I'm afraid to pray out loud? Do I have to?
But you, when you pray, go into your room, and when you have shut your door, pray to your Father who is in the secret place; and your Father who sees in secret will reward you openly (Matthew 6:6).

Where is God when I don't understand why people say, "In Jesus' name," as they end a prayer?
You did not choose Me, but I chose you and appointed you that you should go and bear fruit, and that your fruit should remain, that whatever you ask the Father in My name He may give you (John 15:16).

Where is God when I wonder how often I should pray?
Pray without ceasing (1 Thessalonians 5:17).

Where is God when I want to know if Jesus ever prayed?
Now it came to pass in those days that He went out to the mountain to pray, and continued all night in prayer to God (Luke 6:12).

Chapter FOUR

Friendly Fire

IT HAPPENED IN the Vietnam War. In the Panama invasion. And in the Persian Gulf War, too. *Friendly fire*. Getting shot at by the enemy is to be expected, but what about getting blasted by the people who are supposed to be on your side?

There is a good chance you've been a victim or at least a target of friendly fire. In friendships it happens all the time: a bayonet in the back, verbal assaults, land mines packed with explosive lies, Stinger missile misunderstandings, hand-to-hand combat.

Where is God when you've been hit by friendly fire? Whether you have a whole school full of friends or you've experienced the shell shock of being blown to bits by friendly fire, this chapter is designed to let you know that God is interested in you and your friendships.

When You're in a Fight

(Friendship Battles)

Friends fight. Some fight dirty and some fight clean, but God understands that friends, even the best of friends, get into arguments, disagreements, squabbles, and fifteen-round knockout matches. When you're going at it with a friend, remember that what you do and say can permanently damage your friendship. The reason for a fight or what actually happens in a fight isn't as important as what happens after the fight.

Where is God when my best friend lies to me? Does Jesus understand the hurt I feel?
Even my own familiar friend in whom I trusted, who ate my bread, has lifted up his heel against me (Psalm 41:9).

Where is God when my friends and I argue all the time?
Finally, all of you be of one mind, having compassion for one another; love as brothers, be tenderhearted, be courteous (1 Peter 3:8).

Where is God when I've been betrayed by a good friend? Does Jesus understand?
But Jesus said to him, "Friend, why have you come?" Then they came and laid hands on Jesus and took Him (Matthew 26:50).

Where is God when I'm having a hard time loving a friend who hurt me?
If someone says, "I love God," and hates his brother, he is a liar (1 John 4:20).

Where is God when I've said some things I shouldn't have and I've ruined a good friendship? What can I do to restore it?
Repent therefore and be converted, that your sins may be blotted out, so that times of refreshing may come from the presence of the Lord (Acts 3:19).

Where is God when a friend keeps stabbing me in the back?
Then Peter came to Him and said, "Lord, how often shall my brother sin against me, and I forgive him? Up to seven times?" Jesus said to him, "I do not say to you, up to seven times, but up to seventy times seven" (Matthew 18:21–22).

Where is God when my friend's love for me is conditional? She's always saying, "Well, if you were really my friend . . ."
The righteous should choose his friends carefully, for the way of the wicked leads them astray (Proverbs 12:26).

Where is God when my best friend hurt me and I'm holding a grudge against him?

Bearing with one another, and forgiving one another, if anyone has a complaint against another; even as Christ forgave you, so you also must do (Colossians 3:13).

Where is God when my friend keeps digging up issues and problems of the past that I can't change? Does it say somewhere that God doesn't remember our sins?
I, even I, am He who blots out your transgressions for My own sake; and I will not remember your sins (Isaiah 43:25).

How to Have a Friend for Life

Having a friend for life is a rare treasure. And the discovery of a loyal friend is worth more than a pirate's bounty. Unfortunately, many friendships aren't worth a rusty nail. Here are some long-lost qualities you can develop to unlock the hidden world of lasting friendships:

- **Realness.** A friend who is real is the type of friend you can see through. He doesn't wear masks or try to be someone he isn't.
- **Risk taking.** A friend who takes risks will get in your face when you're blowing it. A risk-taking friend always looks out for your best interests, not her own. If she looks foolish so you can look good, that's a risk she's willing to take.
- **Responsibleness.** A responsible friend has a growing understanding of what builds up (and blows up) friendships. A responsible friend understands the word *consequence,* that is, "for every action there is a reaction." A responsible friend has figured out what happens when you mix drinking and driving and the hormonal juices of X and Y chromosome bodies.
- **Reliableness.** "We all need somebody we can lean on!" Don't ask me to sing the song *(dial 1-800-IAM-LAME if you want to hear me kill any good song),* but a reliable friend is someone you can lean on. And no matter how hard you lean on a reliable friend, he'll still be standing when others have fallen flat on their faces.

Friendship Frustrations

(Struggles with Friends)

Don't you hate it when some class clown drags his fingernails down the chalkboard? *Ssscrrreeech!* Frustrations in friendships are a lot like that. They're often temporary, but they can make your spine wanna jump out of your back. Frustrations left unsettled will continue to grate and grind on your nerves until you talk to your friend and deal with the problem. Here's some perspective on dealing with the tensions and troubles that come through friendships.

Where is God when my friend pays the tab for everyone anytime we go out?
Wealth makes many friends, but the poor is separated from his friend (Proverbs 19:4).

Where is God when I have a Christian friend who's very selfish?
Whoever exalts himself will be humbled, and he who humbles himself will be exalted (Luke 14:11).

Where is God when I want to find a friend who can keep a secret?
A talebearer reveals secrets, but he who is of a faithful spirit conceals a matter (Proverbs 11:13).

Where is God when I need to know His peace in my struggles with my friends?
In the world you will have tribulation; but be of good cheer, I have overcome the world (John 16:33).

Where is God when my friend has little habits that bug me?
The discretion of a man makes him slow to anger, and his glory is to overlook a transgression (Proverbs 19:11).

Where is God when I've discovered that a very good friend has some deep problems he's been hiding from me?

A friend loves at all times, and a brother is born for adversity (Proverbs 17:17).

Where is God when I have trouble with my temper?
"Be angry, and do not sin": do not let the sun go down on your wrath, nor give place to the devil (Ephesians 4:26–27).

Where is God when I want to know if Jesus' disciples ever experienced tension in their friendship with one another?
And when the ten heard it, they began to be greatly displeased with James and John (Mark 10:41).

Where is God when I have two "best friends," but the three of us are always fighting over one another?
Therefore if there is any consolation in Christ, if any comfort of love, if any fellowship of the Spirit, if any affection and mercy, fulfill my joy by being like-minded, having the same love, being of one accord, of one mind (Philippians 2:1–2).

Where is God when I have a friend who's very inconsiderate?
Moreover if your brother sins against you, go and tell him his fault between you and him alone. If he hears you, you have gained your brother (Matthew 18:15).

Friendship with God

(The Ultimate Friend)

God is the ultimate friend. He will never let you down, never change, never talk behind your back, and never ask you for gas money. His love for you is so strong that nothing can overcome it. You can be yourself completely when you're hanging out with God.

Where is God when I want to be sure that He will always be my friend?
The Lord has appeared of old to me, saying: "Yes, I have loved you

with an everlasting love; therefore with lovingkindness I have drawn you" (Jeremiah 31:3).

Where is God when I wonder if He's with me?
When you pass through the waters, I will be with you; and through the rivers, they shall not overflow you. When you walk through the fire, you shall not be burned, nor shall the flame scorch you (Isaiah 43:2).

Where is God when I wonder if He understands friendship? Did God ever have friends?
And the Scripture was fulfilled which says, "Abraham believed God, and it was accounted to him for righteousness." And he was called the friend of God (James 2:23).

Where is God when I want to know the true extent of His love for me?
Greater love has no one than this, than to lay down one's life for his friends (John 15:13).

Where is God when I've heard that either you're His friend or you're not?
Adulterers and adulteresses! Do you not know that friendship with the world is enmity with God? Whoever therefore wants to be a friend of the world makes himself an enemy of God (James 4:4).

Where is God when I want to know if Jesus ever called anyone His friend?
No longer do I call you servants, for a servant does not know what his master is doing; but I have called you friends, for all things that I heard from My Father I have made known to you (John 15:15).

Where is God when I want to know what God expects out of my friendship with Him?
You are My friends if you do whatever I command you (John 15:14).

Where is God when I want to know how He shows that He's my friend?

But God demonstrates His own love toward us, in that while we were still sinners, Christ died for us (Romans 5:8).

Where is God when I'm not a very good friend to Him?
I acknowledged my sin to You, and my iniquity I have not hidden. I said, "I will confess my transgressions to the LORD," and You forgave the iniquity of my sin (Psalm 32:5).

Stuck in the Trap of Loneliness

(Being Lonely)

Being lonely has often been compared to being stranded on a deserted island. Wrong. Deserted islands still have water, coconuts, and little thatched huts you can sit under (if you know how to build them). Being lonely (even though you have friends) is like snaring yourself in a bear trap. Loneliness is a problem anyone can step into, but when it's your foot that's stuck in the trap, no one feels the pain but you. Being stuck in the trap of loneliness can expose nerves and cause you just enough pain to never want to get close to anybody again. God has a lot to say about loneliness. He understands your thoughts and feelings better than anyone else.

Where is God when as hard as I try, I just don't seem to fit in?
For I know the thoughts that I think toward you, says the LORD, thoughts of peace and not of evil, to give you a future and a hope (Jeremiah 29:11).

Where is God when I've recently moved to a new town and I don't have any friends?
No man shall be able to stand before you all the days of your life; as I was with Moses, so I will be with you. I will not leave you nor forsake you (Joshua 1:5).

Where is God when I feel socially out of it?

And those members of the body which we think to be less honorable, on these we bestow greater honor; and our unpresentable parts have greater modesty (1 Corinthians 12:23).

Where is God when I'm often by myself? Did Jesus ever feel lonely?
And about the ninth hour Jesus cried out with a loud voice, saying, "Eli, Eli, lama sabachthani?" that is, "My God, My God, why have You forsaken Me?" (Matthew 27:46).

Where is God when I want to choose the right type of friends?
But seek first the kingdom of God and His righteousness, and all these things shall be added to you (Matthew 6:33).

Where is God when I'm told the reason I don't have very many friends is that I'm too shy? Did God know what He was doing when He made me?
But now, thus says the LORD, who created you, O Jacob, and He who formed you, O Israel: "Fear not, for I have redeemed you; I have called you by your name; you are Mine" (Isaiah 43:1).

Where is God when I need to know that I'm not the only one who's ever been lonely?
Turn Yourself to me, and have mercy on me, for I am desolate and afflicted. The troubles of my heart have enlarged; bring me out of my distresses! (Psalm 25:16–17).

Where is God when I can't seem to find the right type of friends?
Our soul waits for the LORD; He is our help and our shield (Psalm 33:20).

Where is God when the friendships I develop never seem to last?
And not only that, but we also glory in tribulations, knowing that tribulation produces perseverance; and perseverance, character; and character, hope (Romans 5:3–4).

Loving the Unlovables

(Being Like Jesus)

If you've ever been teased, ridiculed, or snubbed by others who thought they were better than you, you know what it's like to feel unlovable. I've got good news for you: *God loves the unlovables. And if you think you're unlovable, God loves you all the more!* Jesus Christ came for people who aren't perfect and know it. If you're a Christian, you've got a mission: Love the unlovables.

Where is God when I sit across from a real jerk in my science class? Does God expect me to actually love him?
And the King will answer and say to them, "Assuredly, I say to you, inasmuch as you did it to one of the least of these My brethren, you did it to Me" (Matthew 25:40).

Where is God when I try to be nice to people who don't have friends, but it seems they could care less about me?
And let us not grow weary while doing good, for in due season we shall reap if we do not lose heart (Galatians 6:9).

Where is God when I have trouble accepting students who aren't very popular?
Be of the same mind toward one another. Do not set your mind on high things, but associate with the humble. Do not be wise in your own opinion (Romans 12:16).

Where is God when I want to know if Jesus faced opposition for hanging out with undesirable people?
The Son of Man came eating and drinking, and they say, "Look, a glutton and a winebibber, a friend of tax collectors and sinners!" But wisdom is justified by her children (Matthew 11:19).

Where is God when I know so many people on my campus who don't have friends?

The LORD is near to those who have a broken heart, and saves such as have a contrite spirit (Psalm 34:18).

Where is God when I want to develop a Christlike attitude toward needy people?

The Spirit of the Lord GOD is upon Me, because the LORD has anointed Me to preach good tidings to the poor; He has sent Me to heal the brokenhearted, to proclaim liberty to the captives, and the opening of the prison to those who are bound (Isaiah 61:1).

Where is God when my youth pastor talks about reaching out to students who don't have any friends?

Walk in wisdom toward those who are outside, redeeming the time. Let your speech always be with grace, seasoned with salt, that you may know how you ought to answer each one (Colossians 4:5-6).

Where is God when it seems that so many students lack compassion these days?

But when He saw the multitudes, He was moved with compassion for them, because they were weary and scattered, like sheep having no shepherd (Matthew 9:36-38).

Where is God when I want to explain to a friend who got dumped by her boyfriend that God understands her loneliness?

He heals the brokenhearted and binds up their wounds (Psalm 147:3).

How to Lose a Friend

This may sound crazy, but I want to help you lose a friend. Possibly more than one. Answer this question: Are your friends pulling you up, or are they dragging you down? If they're pulling you up, you're a winner, and you've got what other kids are dying for. But if your friends are pulling you down, you're

- on a sinking ship.
- standing under a dying elephant.
- going down a paddle without a river

- playing with dynamite.
- lighting the fuse of your dynamite.
- in deep yogurt.

If you think it's time to let go and move on to healthier, positive friendships, here are some practical, creative ways to say *adios, ciao,* and bye-bye:

- Move (send no forwarding address).
- Write a letter. Let her know how you feel.
- Play Paper, Rock, Scissors to see who goes to a different school.
- Politely decline invitations to parties.
- Let him know that *you* have decided to make some changes.
- Shave your head, refuse to shower, and chant, "Snodgrass, snodgrass."
- Tell your friend the truth. (This friendship isn't working.)

Putting Up with Peer Pressure

(Taking a Stand)

Peer pressure is a lot like gravity: No matter how hard you try to jump away from it, it's always going to have a pull on you. Even if you don't give in to the 1,001 faces and forms of peer pressure, it will affect you and your decisions. God's Word has loads to say about who you hang out with and why. Why not take His advice and learn that God's way is the easy way (does that sound like Mom and Dad or what)?

Where is God when my friends are always trying to get me to cheat for them?

Blessed is the man who walks not in the counsel of the ungodly, nor stands in the path of sinners, nor sits in the seat of the scornful; but his delight is in the law of the LORD, and in His law he meditates day and night (Psalm 1:1–2).

Where is God when I love my friends, but because I'm not into partying like they are, they don't call me on the weekends?
The LORD also will be a refuge for the oppressed, a refuge in times of trouble. And those who know Your name will put their trust in You; for You, LORD, have not forsaken those who seek You (Psalm 9:9–10).

Where is God when I'm tired of trying to impress my friends?
Come to Me, all you who labor and are heavy laden, and I will give you rest (Matthew 11:28).

Where is God when my friends pressure me to use drugs, and I'm so scared I don't know what to do?
Whenever I am afraid, I will trust in You. In God (I will praise His word), in God I have put my trust; I will not fear. What can flesh do to me? (Psalm 56:3–4).

Where is God when I go shopping with my friends and they want me to shoplift?
Do not be deceived: "Evil company corrupts good habits" (1 Corinthians 15:33).

Where is God when I'm faced with choosing between what my friends want and what my parents want?
Children, obey your parents in the Lord, for this is right. "Honor your father and mother," which is the first commandment with promise: "that it may be well with you and you may live long on the earth" (Ephesians 6:1–3).

Where is God when I can't afford the clothes my friends wear, but I want to fit in?
Therefore I say to you, do not worry about your life, what you will eat or what you will drink; nor about your body, what you will put on. Is not life more than food and the body more than clothing? (Matthew 6:25).

Where is God when I feel envious of friends who are popular?
For where envy and self-seeking exist, confusion and every evil thing are there (James 3:16).

Where is God when my friends pressure me to drive as if I were in the Indy 500?
A wise man fears and departs from evil, but a fool rages and is self-confident (Proverbs 14:16).

Reaching Out to Friends

(Helping Friends)

Talking to your friends about your relationship with God may be one of the most difficult things you ever do. If you're like most students, you probably feel like you don't know enough about God or the Bible or Jesus. At the same time, you also may know that Jesus placed a priority on making sure people heard His message. What to do? Remember that when you share with others what God means to you, He starts, continues, and finishes His work in their lives. God wants you to be available, and He will make you capable to do what He wants you to do.

Where is God when I wonder if praying for my friends matters to Him?
Praying always with all prayer and supplication in the Spirit, being watchful to this end with all perseverance and supplication for all the saints (Ephesians 6:18).

Where is God when I've been praying for my friends, but I don't seem to see any change in their lives?
Pray without ceasing (1 Thessalonians 5:17).

Where is God when my friend says that Christians are just a bunch of hypocrites?
My little children, let us not love in word or in tongue, but in deed and in truth (1 John 3:18).

Where is God when my friend says that Jesus is just one of many ways to get to heaven?

Jesus said to him, "I am the way, the truth, and the life. No one comes to the Father except through Me" (John 14:6).

Where is God when my friend thinks that God is out to condemn him?
For God did not send His Son into the world to condemn the world, but that the world through Him might be saved (John 3:17).

Where is God when I'm reluctant to share my faith with my friends because I'm afraid of being rejected?
Do not fear therefore; you are of more value than many sparrows. Therefore whoever confesses Me before men, him I will also confess before My Father who is in heaven (Matthew 10:31–32).

Where is God when my friends make fun of me for being a Christian?
Blessed are those who are persecuted for righteousness' sake, for theirs is the kingdom of heaven (Matthew 5:10).

Where is God when I want to know what to tell a friend who says she has a hard time believing in Someone she can't see?
For we walk by faith, not by sight (2 Corinthians 5:7).

Where is God when my Christian friends don't seem to care about sharing their faith? All they want to do is hang around other Christians.
Preach the word! Be ready in season and out of season. Convince, rebuke, exhort, with all longsuffering and teaching (2 Timothy 4:2).

Taming the Tongue

(Word Power)

"Say that word again and I'll wash your mouth out with soap! You better watch your language!" Our parents tried to pass on their knowledge of the power of the tongue. Sometimes they chose funny ways of doing it. By now, you've probably blown a few soap bubbles of your own.

Nobody needs to tell you that words can build or words can destroy. Your words open the door to your heart. And when that door is left hanging open, everyone can look inside and see who you really are. Taming the tongue is learning when to slam the door shut.

Where is God when I have trouble with a foul mouth?
Neither filthiness, nor foolish talking, nor coarse jesting, which are not fitting, but rather giving of thanks (Ephesians 5:4).

Where is God when I tend to gossip even though I'm a Christian?
If anyone among you thinks he is religious, and does not bridle his tongue but deceives his own heart, this one's religion is useless (James 1:26).

Where is God when the guys I hang out with are always bragging about their sexual exploits? Should I?
Let no corrupt word proceed out of your mouth, but what is good for necessary edification, that it may impart grace to the hearers (Ephesians 4:29).

Where is God when my friend is spreading rumors about me? What should I do?
Brethren, if a man is overtaken in any trespass, you who are spiritual restore such a one in a spirit of gentleness, considering yourself lest you also be tempted (Galatians 6:1).

Where is God when my best friend accuses me of lying to him?
In return for my love they are my accusers, but I give myself to prayer (Psalm 109:4).

Where is God when my friends rip on other people and I don't want to be a part of it?
And have no fellowship with the unfruitful works of darkness, but rather expose them (Ephesians 5:11).

Where is God when my best friend is telling everyone else something I told her in confidence?
And be kind to one another, tenderhearted, forgiving one another, just as God in Christ forgave you (Ephesians 4:32).

Where is God when some girls in my class are always gossiping?
Whoever guards his mouth and tongue keeps his soul from troubles (Proverbs 21:23).

Where is God when someone is spreading an awful rumor about a good friend in order to break up our friendship?
A perverse man sows strife, and a whisperer separates the best of friends (Proverbs 16:28).

True Friendship

(Real Friends)

Let's face it: True friendships are not easily found or made. A lot of people are more interested in themselves than in their friends. True friendships involve taking risks, being real, and being brave enough to get in a friend's face when he's messing up. God took an incredible risk when He demonstrated His friendship to you and me by sending His Son, Jesus, into the world. Jesus offers His friendship to us daily and, by His example, shows us what it takes to be a true friend.

Where is God when a friend confronts me with some personal issues I need to work on?
Faithful are the wounds of a friend, but the kisses of an enemy are deceitful (Proverbs 27:6).

Where is God when I want to know what the Bible says about being a trustworthy friend?

A talebearer reveals secrets, but he who is of a faithful spirit conceals a matter (Proverbs 11:13).

Where is God when I need to ask a good friend for advice, but I'm not sure if I should?
Ointment and perfume delight the heart, and the sweetness of a man's friend gives delight by hearty counsel (Proverbs 27:9).

Where is God when I have a friend who's struggling and no one seems to want to help him out?
For if they fall, one will lift up his companion. But woe to him who is alone when he falls, for he has no one to help him up (Ecclesiastes 4:10).

Where is God when I don't know how to help a friend who's depressed all the time?
Now we exhort you, brethren, warn those who are unruly, comfort the fainthearted, uphold the weak, be patient with all (1 Thessalonians 5:14).

Where is God when my friend is in serious trouble?
Is anyone among you suffering? Let him pray (James 5:13).

Where is God when I wonder if it's a good idea for my friends and me to commit our friendships to God?
Then Jonathan said to David, "Go in peace, since we have both sworn in the name of the LORD, saying, 'May the LORD be between you and me, and between your descendants and my descendants, forever'" (1 Samuel 20:42).

Where is God when I want to know what characterizes a really good friendship?
A man who has friends must himself be friendly, but there is a friend who sticks closer than a brother (Proverbs 18:24).

Where is God when I want to learn what it means to be a dependable friend?
Do not forsake your own friend or your father's friend (Proverbs 27:10).

Fanning the Flames of Friendship

(Kick Starting Friendship)

At times in your friendships, things seem flat, common, almost boring. Nothing will spark the fire of your friendships like encouragement. Encouragement sends the roots of your friendships deeper and deeper into the soil of significant and lasting relationships. A high-five, a card in the mail, a crazy message left on an answering machine, and an "I Love You" written in the dirt of a windshield are just a few ways to encourage your friends. God's Word encourages us to be encouragers, people who reflect the God who believes in them.

Where is God when I have a friend who needs to be encouraged?
Therefore comfort each other and edify one another, just as you are also doing (1 Thessalonians 5:11).

Where is God when I want to thank Him for giving me great friends?
Every good gift and every perfect gift is from above, and comes down from the Father of lights, with whom there is no variation or shadow of turning (James 1:17).

Where is God when my friend just became a Christian, and I want him to know what the Bible says about his decision?
I say to you that likewise there will be more joy in heaven over one sinner who repents than over ninety-nine just persons who need no repentance (Luke 15:7).

Where is God when I need a verse to encourage my friends in our weekly Bible study?
Now may the God of patience and comfort grant you to be like-minded toward one another, according to Christ Jesus, that you may with one mind and one mouth glorify the God and Father of our Lord Jesus Christ (Romans 15:5-6).

Where is God when I want to help a friend who feels that she has no direction for her life?

Cause me to hear Your lovingkindness in the morning, for in You do I trust; cause me to know the way in which I should walk, for I lift up my soul to You (Psalm 143:8).

Where is God when I have a friend who's lazy about coming to church?

Not forsaking the assembling of ourselves together, as is the manner of some, but exhorting one another, and so much the more as you see the Day approaching (Hebrews 10:25).

Where is God when my friend and I have had some rocky times together, but we're committed to making our friendship last?

Beloved, let us love one another, for love is of God; and everyone who loves is born of God and knows God (1 John 4:7).

Where is God when my Christian friends and I want to make a stand for Christ in everything we do?

By this all will know that you are My disciples, if you have love for one another (John 13:35).

Where is God when I need His direction in being a good friend?

Teach me to do Your will, for You are my God; Your Spirit is good. Lead me in the land of uprightness (Psalm 143:10).

Chapter FIVE

God's Body Language

BODY. CUERPO. CORPS. Shintsai. Kah-RAH-dah. No matter what language you speak or what country you come from, God wants your body. It doesn't matter if you're a high-school prom queen or a skinny freshman. God wants your body. Pretty weird concept, huh?

You see, God created your body; therefore, the ownership is really His. But it's a gift He's handed over to you to use, grow, stretch the skin out, and comb the hair. Actually, your body is both a gift and a loan because you'll have to turn it in whenever God asks for it back. If you want to be all that God wants you to be in life, give your body back to Him so you can experience all the wonderful plans and purposes He has created for you.

Fortunately, God has given us His Word, the Bible, to communicate a very clear message about what to do with our bodies and why. God wants us to give Him our bodies as an act of worship. Giving God your body is one of the most important things you can do because God's Son, Jesus Christ, gave His body to be crucified so that we might have life through Him. If God has you and your body, you'll be able to experience His language of love for your life.

All this talk about bodies is meaningless unless we discuss sex. God is very interested in your sex life. God is not a cosmic Peeping Tom but a loving Father who's concerned about your sexual decisions. He knows that the sexual decisions you make today will affect the rest of your life. God wants you to have a long and satisfying life *(that includes a satisfying sex life),* but that depends on you and your sexual decisions. You can honor God with your body by making positive sexual decisions.

Too many young people have unnecessary pain from experiencing broken relationships, going too far too soon, or not knowing when to tell a date, "STOP!" God knows that your body can seem like it's going out of control, but just when you think you can't control yourself, He will give you the strength to make the choice that says, "Sorry, you can't have my body. It isn't mine. I gave it to God."

How Far Is Too Far?

(Sexual Choices)

The burning question in dating relationships is, How far is too far? This is a very honest and relevant question for young people who are interested in pleasing God. It's also a very dangerous question because once you've figured out how far is too far in a physical relationship, there's always the pull of your sexual feelings to go *just a little farther*. The Bible won't tell you how far is too far for every situation you are involved in; however, it gives specific guidelines for honoring God and the person you care about. Instead of thinking, *How far can I go in my relationship?* you may want to consider how you can honor God in the dating relationship.

Where is God when I went too far sexually and I feel awful? Will God forgive me?
I, even I, am He who blots out your transgressions for My own sake; and I will not remember your sins (Isaiah 43:25).

Where is God when I want to know why I should wait to be sexually active until I'm married?
Marriage is honorable among all, and the bed undefiled; but fornicators and adulterers God will judge (Hebrews 13:4).

Where is God when I'm so hungry for affection that I let guys take advantage of me?

That each of you should know how to possess his own vessel in sanctification and honor, not in passion of lust, like the Gentiles who do not know God; that no one should take advantage of and defraud his brother in this matter, because the Lord is the avenger of all such, as we also forewarned you and testified (1 Thessalonians 4:4–6).

Where is God when I get so confused between God's standards and the world's standards?

Let no one deceive himself. If anyone among you seems to be wise in this age, let him become a fool that he may become wise (1 Corinthians 3:18).

Where is God when my girlfriend and I are sexually active?

Or do you not know that your body is the temple of the Holy Spirit who is in you, whom you have from God, and you are not your own? For you were bought at a price; therefore glorify God in your body and in your spirit, which are God's (1 Corinthians 6:19–20).

Where is God when I need His forgiveness for making wrong sexual choices?

My little children, these things I write to you, so that you may not sin. And if anyone sins, we have an Advocate with the Father, Jesus Christ the righteous. And He Himself is the propitiation for our sins, and not for ours only but also for the whole world (1 John 2:1–2).

Where is God when my boyfriend and I are making sexual decisions that can have severe consequences?

Likewise you also, reckon yourselves to be dead indeed to sin, but alive to God in Christ Jesus our Lord. Therefore do not let sin reign in your mortal body, that you should obey it in its lusts (Romans 6:11–12).

Where is God when I think the Bible says that only sexual intercourse is wrong?

You have heard that it was said to those of old, "You shall not commit adultery." But I say to you that whoever looks at a woman to lust for her has already committed adultery with her in his heart (Matthew 5:27–28).

Where is God when I want to know the basic guideline for making sexual decisions?
You shall love the LORD your God with all your heart, with all your soul, and with all your strength. And these words which I command you today shall be in your heart (Deuteronomy 6:5–6).

The Lust Buster
Controlling Your Thought Life Before It Controls You

Lust, that seemingly uncontrollable desire to possess something that isn't yours, can haunt, frustrate, break, pursue, and tear down the Christlike character God wants to develop in you. When you see a beautiful person, lust doesn't have to consume your every thought or wildest fantasy. Having good training and knowing your escape route to God when you see trouble coming will help you live a life of purity and obedience. Some of these lust-buster ideas may help you. OK, even if they're stupid, at least they'll get your mind off lust.

- Do your homework.
- Cancel your cable TV subscription.
- Roll in the snow.
- Take a cold shower after rolling in the snow.
- Find a friend who can hold you accountable.
- Look the other way.
- Pray (read that again).
- Avoid places that sell pornography.
- Write a letter to a friend.
- Take up a new sport like bungee jumping, bronco riding, or shark fishing.
- See what God's Word has to say about love, lust, sex, and thought life.

- Become a vegetarian cave dweller.
- Hang out with friends who pull you up instead of down.
- Ask *Sports Illustrated* to change the swimsuit edition to a gorilla suit edition.
- Buy a pair of horse blinders.
- Talk with your youth pastor.
- When all else fails, create your own list of lust busters.

The Dating Dilemma

(Dating Struggles)

Dating is a dilemma. You have one or you don't. You get asked out by the guy you don't like, and your friend gets asked out by the guy you do like. Your date says she's starving, orders an expensive dinner, and then nibbles at it. The guy who picks you up is either too early or too late. Sometimes you never know what to say, or your date talks only about himself. The pressure to date and the pressure of not having a date can be overwhelming. *But did you know that the majority of teens never have their first date until they're out of high school?*

Dating can be difficult, but it can also be a lot of fun as you get to know someone better. Dating can build wonderful memories, but it's also the reason for many heartbreaks. God wants you to develop healthy, positive friendships with members of the opposite sex.

Where is God when my first date was a horrible experience? What should I do if he asks me out again?
Flee, save your lives! And be like the juniper in the wilderness (Jeremiah 48:6).

Where is God when I ask a girl out for a date and I get rejected? Will God reject me, too?

Blessed be God, who has not turned away my prayer, nor His mercy from me! (Psalm 66:20).

Where is God when no one asks me to the prom? Doesn't He realize how important this event is to me?

And those who know Your name will put their trust in You; for You, LORD, have not forsaken those who seek You (Psalm 9:10).

Where is God when I've wanted to break up with my boyfriend for a long time, but I'm afraid to?

Be strong and of good courage, do not fear nor be afraid of them; for the LORD your God, He is the One who goes with you. He will not leave you nor forsake you (Deuteronomy 31:6).

Where is God when my girlfriend and I are kissing and our braces lock?

Set a guard, O LORD, over my mouth; keep watch over the door of my lips (Psalm 141:3).

Where is God when I want to break up with my girlfriend, but I don't know how I can say it without sounding like a fool?

The words of a wise man's mouth are gracious, but the lips of a fool shall swallow him up (Ecclesiastes 10:12).

Where is God when I want to know how I can please Him in my dating relationships?

So that He may establish your hearts blameless in holiness before our God and Father at the coming of our Lord Jesus Christ with all His saints. Finally then, brethren, we urge and exhort in the Lord Jesus that you should abound more and more (1 Thessalonians 3:13; 4:1).

Where is God when I constantly need a boyfriend to cover up my insecurities? How can I find my security in God?

Finally, my brethren, be strong in the Lord and in the power of His might (Ephesians 6:10).

Where is God when I really like a girl and want to date her, but she's not a Christian?

Walk in wisdom toward those who are outside, redeeming the time. Let your speech always be with grace, seasoned with salt, that you may know how you ought to answer each one (Colossians 4:5-6).

Where is God when my friend has a boyfriend and she never spends time with me?
Cast your burden on the LORD, and He shall sustain you; He shall never permit the righteous to be moved (Psalm 55:22).

Where is God when the girl I'm dating is becoming very possessive?
Keep your heart with all diligence, for out of it spring the issues of life (Proverbs 4:23).

True Love Checklist

How do you know if someone really loves you? How can you be sure the person is interested in you as an individual and not as a possession or prize? The best definition of true love can be found in God's love letter to you and me: the Bible. Before you start doing backflips over someone you think you're in love with, look for the following qualities in the person's life.

Read 1 Corinthians 13 and then answer these questions:

- **Love is patient**. Is this person easily upset? What happens when things go wrong?
- **Love is kind**. What do other people say about this person? Is he (or she) cruel? Is he (or she) considerate of you and others?
- **Love does not envy**. How jealous does this person get? Does she (or he) get mad if you talk to other people? Is *Fatal Attraction* a favorite movie?
- **Love does not boast**. Does this person brag a lot? Is he (or she) interested in you or himself (or herself)? Does he (or she) live for God's glory or his (or her) own glory?
- **Love is not proud**. Can this person admit faults? Does she (or he) always have to get the last word? Can she (or he) compromise?

- **Love is not rude**. Does this person's belching make you retch? Does he (or she) make gross remarks all the time?
- **Love is not self-seeking**. Is this person selfish or selfless? Is she (or he) authentically interested in what's best for you?
- **Love is not provoked**. How short is this person's fuse? Does he (or she) get out of control in arguments? Does he (or she) leave holes in walls? Slam doors?
- **Love keeps no record of wrongs**. Does this person refer to past fights? When you say, "I'm sorry," are you forgiven?
- **Love does not delight in evil**. Does this person hate evil? Is he (or she) a lover of what is good?
- **Love rejoices in truth**. Is this person a liar? Does she (or he) have a reputation for not telling the truth? Does she (or he) hide secrets? Would others say she (or he) is honest?
- **Love always protects**. If the two of you were robbed, would this person give up the wallet or use you for a shield? Does this person give you a sense of security?
- **Love always trusts**. Can you share secrets with this person without fearing he (or she) will tell everyone else?
- **Love always hopes**. Is this person optimistic or pessimistic? Does she (or he) have confidence in a personal relationship with God?
- **Love always perseveres**. Does this person face or run from problems? Can he (or she) handle conflict in a relationship?
- **Love never fails**. Is this person a quitter? Is she (or he) crushed by failure, or does she (or he) try to learn something from it? Has she (or he) ever successfully defused a hand grenade?

Parental Guidance Recommended

(Advice from Parents)

Don't you wish you had cool parents who would let you do *anything* you want? Do you ever wonder if your parents will ever stop being so overprotective? God knows that even though parents make mistakes, they can help you avoid heartaches by helping you learn to make good choices. Dating is just one of the areas in which your parents may be interested in helping you make sound decisions. (Parental Guidance Comic Relief Idea #4,874: Imagine your folks on their very first date. Re-create the comedy and romance of this momentous occasion on a videotape and give it to them for their anniversary.)

Where is God when my parents constantly lecture me about who I date?

Listen to counsel and receive instruction, that you may be wise in your latter days (Proverbs 19:20).

Where is God when I'm angry because my parents make me come home earlier on dates than my brother?

A fool vents all his feelings, but a wise man holds them back (Proverbs 29:11).

Where is God when my parents embarrass me every time my girlfriend is over? What can I tell my parents to make them stop?

Fathers, do not provoke your children, lest they become discouraged (Colossians 3:21).

Where is God when my old-fashioned parents refuse to let me date before I'm sixteen?

Listen to your father who begot you, and do not despise your mother when she is old (Proverbs 23:22).

Where is God when my mom, who is single, seems more concerned about her love life than me?

Can a woman forget her nursing child, and not have compassion on the son of her womb? Surely they may forget, yet I will not forget you (Isaiah 49:15).

Where is God when my parents catch my boyfriend and me kissing in the den? What do I say?

His left hand is under my head, and his right hand embraces me (Song of Solomon 8:3).

Where is God when I want to date someone who isn't a Christian, but my parents won't let me?
Children, obey your parents in all things, for this is well pleasing to the Lord (Colossians 3:20).

Where is God when my dad had an affair and I'm afraid I'll do the same someday?
Let your fountain be blessed, and rejoice with the wife of your youth. As a loving deer and a graceful doe, let her breasts satisfy you at all times; and always be enraptured with her love (Proverbs 5:18–19).

Beauty from the Inside Out

(Inner Beauty)

Beauty isn't all it's cracked up to be. In our society, beauty is considered important. Beauty sells. It'll get you dates. If you've been born with it, it's absolutely free, and with a little care, it'll last almost three-fourths a lifetime. However, too much significance is placed on outward beauty.

The real gem that most people miss is inner beauty. The image you see in the mirror is a mere reflection of who God has created you to be. God is more interested in how beautiful you are on the inside than how you look compared to someone on a magazine cover. You are precious and special to God. He sees beauty from the inside out.

Where is God when I secretly despise the popular "beautiful" people at school?
A sound heart is life to the body, but envy is rottenness to the bones (Proverbs 14:30).

Where is God when I want to know if I'm any less important than others because I think I don't look as good?

But from those who seemed to be something—whatever they were, it makes no difference to me; God shows personal favoritism to no man—for those who seemed to be something added nothing to me (Galatians 2:6).

Where is God when I wish I were stronger and had better muscles?

My flesh and my heart fail; but God is the strength of my heart and my portion forever (Psalm 73:26).

Where is God when I'm embarrassed to change my clothes in the locker room? Did anyone else ever feel this way?

Then the eyes of both of them were opened, and they knew that they were naked; and they sewed fig leaves together and made themselves coverings (Genesis 3:7).

Where is God when I want to know if He can relate to feeling unattractive?

Just as many were astonished at you, so His visage was marred more than any man, and His form more than the sons of men (Isaiah 52:14).

Where is God when I feel I can never measure up to the people in movies and magazines?

But now, thus says the LORD, who created you, O Jacob, and He who formed you, O Israel: "Fear not, for I have redeemed you; I have called you by your name; you are Mine" (Isaiah 43:1).

Where is God when my friends are caught up in their clothes and hairstyles?

Therefore I say to you, do not worry about your life, what you will eat or what you will drink; nor about your body, what you will put on. Is not life more than food and the body more than clothing? (Matthew 6:25).

Where is God when I want to know what I can do to develop inner beauty?

Charm is deceitful and beauty is passing, but a woman who fears the LORD, she shall be praised (Proverbs 31:30).

The Love Connection

(Real Love)

Didn't a patriot from the past say, "Give me love or give me death"? Or was it Kennedy who said, "Don't ask yourself what love can do for you, but what you can do for love"? And didn't Martin Luther King, Jr., say, "I have a . . . love"? My brain synapses don't connect too often, but that's even more common when people talk about love. The brain and the emotions usually don't have much in common when it comes to love. One is interested in logic; the other, PASSION.

God has wired you with a heart that is capable of giving and receiving love. The only problem is that there's so much confusion over what true love is and what it isn't. To plug you into the right connection so you can best understand what true love is, God's Word gives a specific look at the life of Jesus Christ. Jesus Christ describes God's outpouring of love for a lost and hurting world. That's a connection you won't want to miss in the people you care about.

Where is God when I wonder what real love is all about?
In this is love, not that we loved God, but that He loved us and sent His Son to be the propitiation for our sins (1 John 4:10).

Where is God when I want to tell if a guy really loves me?
Let nothing be done through selfish ambition or conceit, but in lowliness of mind let each esteem others better than himself (Philippians 2:3).

Where is God when I want to know the difference between love and infatuation?

Love suffers long and is kind; love does not envy; love does not parade itself, is not puffed up; does not behave rudely, does not seek its own, is not provoked, thinks no evil (1 Corinthians 13:4–5).

Where is God when I want to know if there is a difference between His love and human love?
Beloved, let us love one another, for love is of God; and everyone who loves is born of God and knows God. He who does not love does not know God, for God is love (1 John 4:7–8).

Where is God when I want to love a person without having to express my love physically?
My little children, let us not love in word or in tongue, but in deed and in truth (1 John 3:18).

Where is God when I wonder how love can be both so powerful and so mysterious?
Set me as a seal upon your heart, as a seal upon your arm; for love is as strong as death, jealousy as cruel as the grave; its flames are flames of fire, a most vehement flame (Song of Solomon 8:6).

Where is God when I want to learn to love others as God loves them?
By this we know that we love the children of God, when we love God and keep His commandments (1 John 5:2).

Where is God when I want my love life to be filled with romance, passion, and mystery? Is this an unreal expectation?
Therefore do not be unwise, but understand what the will of the Lord is (Ephesians 5:17).

Where is God when I can't see the connection between God's love and Jesus Christ?
But God demonstrates His own love toward us, in that while we were still sinners, Christ died for us (Romans 5:8).

Where is God when I want to know why I can't express my love physically to my girlfriend if I truly love her?

But fornication and all uncleanness or covetousness, let it not even be named among you, as is fitting for saints (Ephesians 5:3).

Where is God when my feelings seem to take control of my love life?
Search me, O God, and know my heart; try me, and know my anxieties (Psalm 139:23).

Making Purity a Priority

(Personal Purity)

You live in a world obsessed with sexuality. Yet if you're a Christian, you walk with *the* God who is holy. That means pure. There's nothing evil, rotten, blotched, stained, or ugly about who He is. Being pure means being without sin. Because God loves us so much and wants the absolute best for us, He wants us to lead sinless lives so we can reflect His holiness. A big step in growing closer to God is making purity a priority in your life. Why? "Blessed are the pure in heart, for they shall see God" (Matthew 5:8).

Where is God when I think sex is dirty and bad?
So God created man in His own image; in the image of God He created him; male and female He created them. Then God saw everything that He had made, and indeed it was very good. So the evening and the morning were the sixth day (Genesis 1:27, 31).

Where is God when I've earned a reputation on campus for being "easy"?
Therefore put to death your members which are on the earth: fornication, uncleanness, passion, evil desire, and covetousness, which is idolatry (Colossians 3:5).

Where is God when I wonder why He wants me to be obedient in the area of personal purity?

Pursue peace with all people, and holiness, without which no one will see the Lord (Hebrews 12:14).

Where is God when I want to know what He has to say about personal purity?
Flee also youthful lusts; but pursue righteousness, faith, love, peace with those who call on the Lord out of a pure heart (2 Timothy 2:22).

Where is God when I want to keep my focus on Him in a world so focused on sex?
Looking unto Jesus, the author and finisher of our faith, who for the joy that was set before Him endured the cross, despising the shame, and has sat down at the right hand of the throne of God (Hebrews 12:2).

Where is God when I want to know God's will for my body?
I beseech you therefore, brethren, by the mercies of God, that you present your bodies a living sacrifice, holy, acceptable to God, which is your reasonable service (Romans 12:1).

Where is God when I wonder what God's holiness and my sexual decisions have in common?
For this is the will of God, your sanctification: that you should abstain from sexual immorality (1 Thessalonians 4:3).

Where is God when I know so many Christians who are sexually active? Why shouldn't I be like them?
The righteousness of the upright will deliver them, but the unfaithful will be caught by their lust (Proverbs 11:6).

Where is God when I wonder if He will honor my desire to be pure like Him?
Blessed are the pure in heart, for they shall see God (Matthew 5:8).

Where is God when I'm easy prey to peer pressure?
Do not lay hands on anyone hastily, nor share in other people's sins; keep yourself pure (1 Timothy 5:22).

Where is God when I get so discouraged trying to be pure like God wants me to be?
And everyone who has this hope in Him purifies himself, just as He is pure (1 John 3:3).

Mental Madness

(Living without Lust)

Lust is mental madness. It takes something that God created as good and reduces it to a selfish, possessive act. If you've struggled or are struggling with your thought life, there is hope. We serve a God who is forgiving and patient. He is able to help you with any problem, no matter how large it is or how crazy it makes you. You can have control over your thought life because God will not let you be tempted beyond what you can handle (1 Corinthians 10:13).

Where is God when I feel guilty about my sexual thoughts?
And by this we know that we are of the truth, and shall assure our hearts before Him. For if our heart condemns us, God is greater than our heart, and knows all things (1 John 3:19–20).

Where is God when I see a girl at the beach and I have to control what goes through my mind?
I have made a covenant with my eyes; why then should I look upon a young woman? (Job 31:1).

Where is God when I find it tough not to be influenced by this world and its perspective on sexuality?
For all that is in the world—the lust of the flesh, the lust of the eyes, and the pride of life—is not of the Father but is of the world (1 John 2:16).

Where is God when the media influences me concerning sex?
Now I am no longer in the world, but these are in the world, and I

come to You. Holy Father, keep through Your name those whom You have given Me, that they may be one as We are (John 17:11).

Where is God when I need to know what He says about sexual immorality?

Flee sexual immorality. Every sin that a man does is outside the body, but he who commits sexual immorality sins against his own body (1 Corinthians 6:18).

Where is God when I'm struggling with lust?

How can a young man cleanse his way? By taking heed according to Your word (Psalm 119:9).

Where is God when He is responsible for giving me major doses of testosterone?

Therefore do not let sin reign in your mortal body, that you should obey it in its lusts. And do not present your members as instruments of unrighteousness to sin, but present yourselves to God as being alive from the dead, and your members as instruments of righteousness to God (Romans 6:12–13).

Where is God when I'm having trouble with my thought life?

Finally, brethren, whatever things are true, whatever things are noble, whatever things are just, whatever things are pure, whatever things are lovely, whatever things are of good report, if there is any virtue and if there is anything praiseworthy—meditate on these things (Philippians 4:8).

Sex and Your Friends

(Peer Pressure)

Dating. Sex. Relationships. Sex. Friendships. Sex is just one of the things that friends normally talk about. *The friends you choose will have a major influence on your sexual decisions*. If your friends are sexually active, you're going to face tough choices. If your friends aren't sexually active, there will probably be less pressure on you to be sexually active.

It works the other way, too. Your friends can get unnecessary pressure taken off them by the positive sexual decisions you choose to make.

Where is God when all my friends brag about the girls they've had sex with?

Blessed is the man who walks not in the counsel of the ungodly, nor stands in the path of sinners, nor sits in the seat of the scornful; but his delight is in the law of the LORD, and in His law he meditates day and night (Psalm 1:1–2).

Where is God when a good friend likes me more than a friend, but I need to tell him that the feeling isn't mutual?

How forceful are right words! But what does your arguing prove? (Job 6:25).

Where is God when my friends are jealous of me because I always go out with beautiful girls?

All my close friends abhor me, and those whom I love have turned against me (Job 19:19).

Where is God when I have a friend who is always dating, but I think she dates so much because she's insecure?

We then who are strong ought to bear with the scruples of the weak, and not to please ourselves (Romans 15:1).

Where is God when my friends try to set me up with someone I don't want to go out with?

So do this, my son, and deliver yourself; for you have come into the hand of your friend: go and humble yourself; plead with your friend (Proverbs 6:3).

Where is God when my friends call me a prude for not being sexually active?

Blessed are you when they revile and persecute you, and say all kinds of evil against you falsely for My sake (Matthew 5:11).

Where is God when I'm concerned about a friend who's involved in a dangerous dating relationship?
Yet do not count him as an enemy, but admonish him as a brother (2 Thessalonians 3:15).

Where is God when my friend was sexually active and other kids in our youth group gossiped about her?
So when they continued asking Him, He raised Himself up and said to them, "He who is without sin among you, let him throw a stone at her first" (John 8:7).

Mere Image

(Outer Beauty)

It's easy to think of appearance and attraction as similar items when you're checking out the dating menu. But before you order, be sure to know that appearance and attraction can be as different as anteaters and auks (diving birds found in the northern seas, with webbed feet and short wings used as paddles). Attraction involves both inner and outer qualities and characteristics that draw other people to you. However, appearance has to do with what you look like on the outside. God is more interested in the attractiveness of your life than the loveliness of your face. And He doesn't want you to be fooled by the mere image of appearance.

Where is God when I'm so frustrated by society's emphasis on how you look and not on who you are?
For the LORD does not see as man sees; for man looks at the outward appearance, but the LORD looks at the heart (1 Samuel 16:7).

Where is God when guys are always telling me I have a great

personality, but no one ever asks me out? How can I be patient?
Wait on the LORD; be of good courage, and He shall strengthen your heart; wait, I say, on the LORD! (Psalm 27:14).

Where is God when I know He didn't make me as good-looking as other teens? What can I do to be beautiful in God's eyes?
Therefore, as the elect of God, holy and beloved, put on tender mercies, kindness, humility, meekness, longsuffering (Colossians 3:12).

Where is God when I'm not overweight like I used to be, but I still feel that way inside? Does God still love me?
"My kindness shall not depart from you, nor shall My covenant of peace be removed," says the LORD, who has mercy on you (Isaiah 54:10).

Where is God when it seems the only way I can get a guy's attention is to wear skimpy clothes?
For those who live according to the flesh set their minds on the things of the flesh, but those who live according to the Spirit, the things of the Spirit (Romans 8:5).

Where is God when I'm tired of trying to compete with others to see who can look the best?
Let us not become conceited, provoking one another, envying one another (Galatians 5:26).

Questions I'm Afraid to Ask

(Tough Questions)

When it comes to asking questions about sex and feeling stupid, you're not alone. Thousands of students have millions upon jillions of questions about their bodies (and other people's bodies).

Here are some tough questions on some difficult subjects that I know many young people wrestle with on a daily basis. I want to emphasize that if you or a friend has been a victim of sexual abuse (incest, rape, date rape, stepparent relationships), you need to get help from someone you can trust. A parent, a youth pastor, a teacher, a counselor, or another caring adult will be able to listen to you.

You do not have to suffer alone with pain and confusion.

Where is God when I'm troubled about a friend who's been sexually abused, and she needs God's strength to tell someone about it?

Fear not, for I am with you; I will bring your descendants from the east, and gather you from the west (Isaiah 43:5).

Where is God when my friend just found out he tested positive for the HIV virus, and he needs God's comfort?

Come to Me, all you who labor and are heavy laden, and I will give you rest. Take My yoke upon you and learn from Me, for I am gentle and lowly in heart, and you will find rest for your souls. For My yoke is easy and My burden is light (Matthew 11:28–30).

Where is God when someone I know recently had an abortion and she hates herself for it?

But now, thus says the LORD, who created you, O Jacob, and He who formed you, O Israel: "Fear not, for I have redeemed you; I have called you by your name; you are Mine. When you pass through the waters, I will be with you; and through the rivers, they shall not overflow you. When you walk through the fire, you shall not be burned, nor shall the flame scorch you" (Isaiah 43:1–2).

Where is God when my best friend's father molested her and I don't know if I can forgive him?

Bearing with one another, and forgiving one another, if anyone has a complaint against another; even as Christ forgave you, so you also must do (Colossians 3:13).

Where is God when a friend tells me he has strong sexual feelings

for people of the same sex? What does the Bible say that will help him?

As the Father loved Me, I also have loved you; abide in My love (John 15:9).

Where is God when my teammate is struggling with wanting to see pornographic magazines, adult movie channels, and porn videos? What does the Bible say?

Do not lust after her beauty in your heart, nor let her allure you with her eyelids (Proverbs 6:25).

Where is God when my friend wants to know why she can't sleep around with anyone she wants?

For God did not call us to uncleanness, but in holiness (1 Thessalonians 4:7).

Where is God when I am troubled about a friend who needs help to overcome some very destructive sexual behaviors?

The troubles of my heart have enlarged; bring me out of my distresses! (Psalm 25:17).

Where is God when my classmate is afraid to go to counseling for her sexual problems? Is counseling a very good idea?

Where there is no counsel, the people fall; but in the multitude of counselors there is safety (Proverbs 11:14).

Where is God when I am trying to help a buddy who feels like he's fighting a losing battle trying to overcome being so promiscuous?

For whatever is born of God overcomes the world. And this is the victory that has overcome the world—our faith (1 John 5:4).

Chapter SIX

Family Frustrations

MOVING BRINGS OUT the worst in me. Packing boxes. Lifting. Grunting. Throwing out stuff I don't need. Leaving old friends. Cleaning. Digging through piles of junk I'd rather just leave as piles of junk. Breaking things. Organizing the unorganizable. Unpacking. Unpacking the piles of junk I reluctantly decided to bring with me. Leery new neighbors staring at me as if I had an antenna on my head. *Hi, my name's George Jetson. What's yours?*

Moving is all about change, and change is what families are all about. Families are in the constant, lifelong process of moving and changing. That's the sign of a healthy family. Change brings about growth, and moving shows progress—if it's in the right direction. Many of today's families are changing and moving in the wrong direction. Divorce. Physical abuse. Emotional abuse. Sexual abuse. Silence. Workaholism. Affairs. Unrealistic expectations. Tragedies. Heading in the wrong direction is a bad move for every family member.

You can help your family head in the right direction by following God's direction for your life. Your family may change—or it may not—but you will move in the right direction. God cares about your family. He cares about you. He wants you to make moves that bring you closer to Him and your family. His Word can help you deal with problems in a constructive way. You are a key part of His family building plan.

Blended Family Blues

(Stepfamilies)

Helping students deal with their parents' divorce and the awkwardness of seeing their parents remarry has been one of my biggest challenges as a youth minister.

Blended families can produce mixed feelings for young people. Stepmoms, stepdads, stepbrothers and stepsisters, stepgrammas— without any decision made on your part, you inherit a whole family of steps. If you're in a blended family, you know the endless issues: holidays, communication, discipline, new ways of doing things, and wondering where you fit in. But catch this one truth: Out of the millions of divorced families, God specifically cares about you and your family.

Where is God when my stepdad seems not to care about me? My father died when I was young. Can God be the dad I don't have?
For you did not receive the spirit of bondage again to fear, but you received the Spirit of adoption by whom we cry out, "Abba, Father." The Spirit Himself bears witness with our spirit that we are children of God (Romans 8:15–16).

Where is God when I have nobody to talk to at my house? Will Jesus hear what I have to say when no one else will?
Now this is the confidence that we have in Him, that if we ask anything according to His will, He hears us (1 John 5:14).

Where is God when my stepfamily is messed up, but nobody is willing to talk about it?
Let us therefore come boldly to the throne of grace, that we may obtain mercy and find grace to help in time of need (Hebrews 4:16).

Where is God when my stepmom can't relate to any of my problems?
I, even I, am He who comforts you. Who are you that you should be

afraid of a man who will die, and of the son of a man who will be made like grass? (Isaiah 51:12).

Where is God when my stepdad never seems to have a positive thing to say to me?
For the LORD has comforted His people, and will have mercy on His afflicted (Isaiah 49:13).

Where is God when I need strength to handle all the hassles in my stepfamily?
Watch, stand fast in the faith, be brave, be strong (1 Corinthians 16:13).

Where is God when I can't stand my stepbrothers?
When a man's ways please the LORD, He makes even his enemies to be at peace with him (Proverbs 16:7).

Where is God when I want to know what I should do to develop a better relationship with my stepmom?
Be at peace among yourselves (1 Thessalonians 5:13).

Where is God when my mom always sides with my stepfather and never sticks up for me?
The LORD is for me among those who help me; therefore I shall see my desire on those who hate me (Psalm 118:7).

Cruel and Unusual Punishment

(Getting Busted)

House arrest. Restriction. Grounded for life. A stiff sentence. Electronic surveillance. You've been nailed for a no-no, and now you've got to pay. Parents have the incredible distinction of playing prosecutor, judge, and jury. They state the alleged crime, present the evidence, listen to the defendant's case, deliberate on a decision, and cast the sentence. The only thing you get to be is the criminal and defense attorney with a losing argument. The defendant is guilty as charged. BAM! Case closed.

Why do parents ground teenagers? I don't have all the answers, but God's Word has some specific reasons for discipline and consequences for making poor decisions. If you're confined to house arrest, His Word can shine some light on your dark, dingy, rat-infested prison cell. (P.S. Don't try to escape. Prisoners have been shot for less than that!)

Where is God when I don't feel like listening to my parents?
Whoever loves instruction loves knowledge, but he who hates correction is stupid (Proverbs 12:1).

Where is God when my friends don't obey their parents and they don't get in trouble? Why should I obey mine?
Children, obey your parents in the Lord, for this is right (Ephesians 6:1).

Where is God when my parents won't let me do anything?
My son, hear the instruction of your father, and do not forsake the law of your mother; for they will be a graceful ornament on your head, and chains about your neck (Proverbs 1:8–9).

Where is God when a friend told me the Bible says, "Obeying my parents is pleasing to God"?
Children, obey your parents in all things, for this is well pleasing to the Lord (Colossians 3:20).

Where is God when I don't understand why parents discipline their kids?
He who spares his rod hates his son, but he who loves him disciplines him promptly (Proverbs 10:17).

Where is God when my dad says I'm supposed to be a good example to my younger brothers and sisters? Why?
He who keeps instruction is in the way of life, but he who refuses correction goes astray (Proverbs 10:17).

Where is God when I see no reason to obey my parents? Do I obey them just because they say so?
Poverty and shame will come to him who disdains correction, but he who regards a rebuke will be honored (Proverbs 13:18).

Where is God when my friend keeps getting in trouble with his folks?
He who disdains instruction despises his own soul, but he who heeds rebuke gets understanding (Proverbs 15:32).

How to Get Permission to Do Just About Anything

When was the last time you were denied permission to go
- to the mall with your friends?
- to see *Bambi Chainsaws Manhattan?*
- to the bathroom?
- to a Wrestlemania Slugfest?
- to Paris for the weekend?
- to an unnamed destination?

If you want to learn how to get permission to do just about anything, like bungee jumping over flaming vats of vegetable oil, read on.

Establish Trust: Earn the Right to Get Permission

There's more to getting the car than bringing it back with gas in the tank. Trust is probably the strongest criterion parents use when giving permission. If you're trustworthy, you're worth trusting. You earn trust by keeping promises, following through on what you said you'd do, and making sure if you break your parents' trust, you own up to it quickly.

Develop Your Game Plan: Know the Five W's (Who, What, When, Why, Where)

Friday Night Scenario #3758496785: Teenager Pleading for House Leave

"Mom, can I go out with Tom tonight?"

"What are you going to do?"

"I don't know. We're supposed to go over to Bob's house."

"Bob who?"

"I don't know. He's a friend of Susan's."

"Susan who?"

"Some girl in Bob's science class."

"Where does Bob live?"

"Somewhere near town."

"You'll have to be a little more specific than that. Which town?"

"The town Bob lives in!"

"When are you going to be home?"

"Before sunrise."

"Forget it."

Answer the Five W's. Whatever you do, answer the Five W's. In most cases, they are your ticket out the door. Forget the Five W's and you'll have to resort to Friday Night Scenario #3758496786: "Mom, can Tom come over tonight?"

Hang Out with Friends Your Parents Trust

Back to the trust issue. If your parents know and like your friends (remember, knowing and liking can be diametrically opposed), you're off to a very good start. If you want to go somewhere for the weekend or out to a party, your parents need to know your friends are trustworthy—trustworthy like you.

Do Your Work (Schoolwork, Chores, Watering the Cat . . . Get It Done!)

"Mom, can I go outside to play?"

"Not until you clean your room."

You've heard it since you were a little kid. You want to do something or go somewhere? Clean your room. Clean the kitchen. Clean the yard. Wash the dog. Scrub the toilets. Do your wash. Finish your homework. Doing your work, whatever the work is, shows your parents that you're a team player. The choice begins with you.

Family Fitness

(Positive Influence)

Are you making your family stronger or weaker? Are you working out to be a team player? Are you a positive, contributing member of your family? Everything you say and everything you do in your family makes a difference. Yes, *everything!* It's easy to forget what a powerful influence you can exert on your family. It's also really easy to forget that attitudes, words, actions, slipups, mistakes, and deliberate acts of unkindness affect how others treat you.

God wants you to be a change maker in your family. God's Word has plenty of character-building carbos for you to feast on so you can make your family stronger. Dig in and get yourself in shape!

Where is God when I want to know how I can help my sister who's going through a hard time?
Exhort one another daily (Hebrews 3:13).

Where is God when I want to be a positive influence in my family and I wonder what I should do?
Therefore comfort each other and edify one another, just as you also are doing (1 Thessalonians 5:11).

Where is God when my parents say my brothers and I fight too much?
Jesus therefore answered and said to them, "Do not murmur among yourselves" (John 6:43).

Where is God when my little sister always wants to spend time with me?
Let each of you look out not only for his own interests, but also for the interests of others (Philippians 2:4).

Where is God when I want to change the way I am at home?
Do all things without complaining and disputing (Philippians 2:14).

Where is God when my mom is depressed about her recent divorce? How can I help her?
A merry heart does good, like medicine, but a broken spirit dries the bones (Proverbs 17:22).

Where is God when I'm trying to learn how to share my clothes with my sister?
So let each one give as he purposes in his heart, not grudgingly or of necessity; for God loves a cheerful giver (2 Corinthians 9:7).

Where is God when I want to show my parents I appreciate all the things they do for me?
Be thankful (Colossians 3:15).

Where is God when I want to develop some positive qualities that will make a difference in my family?
. . . to be subject to rulers and authorities, to obey, to be ready for every good work, to speak evil of no one, to be peaceable, gentle, showing all humility to all men (Titus 3:1–2).

Going Ballistic

(Words That Kill)

Smart weapons rarely miss their targets. Fiber-optic sighting. A tonnage of big bang stuff. A brain kinda like Einstein's. These smart weapons will fly up a Volkswagen tailpipe in Missouri if steered in the right direction. The Persian Gulf War featured the intricate technology and precision of radar-guided missiles. Our words, especially cruel words, are just like smart weapons. Words meant to hurt have destructive power that cripples human targets. What comes out of the mouth can launch aerial attacks right to the heart.

Fortunately, because of Jesus Christ's death and resurrection,

God provides the cleanup crew of grace and forgiveness. Admitting your out-of-control tongue inflicted unnecessary damage is the first step toward healing the wound. God is ready and willing to forgive ballistic blunders. He wants you to be wise with your words so you can target your tongue toward peace.

Where is God when my mouth is always getting me in trouble at home?
The wise in heart will be called prudent, and sweetness of the lips increases learning (Proverbs 16:21).

Where is God when I talk back to my parents?
In the multitude of words sin is not lacking, but he who restrains his lips is wise (Proverbs 10:19).

Where is God when my dad is always telling me to do what he says?
Cease listening to instruction, my son, and you will stray from the words of knowledge (Proverbs 19:27).

Where is God when I never seem to say things in the right way?
A word fitly spoken is like apples of gold in settings of silver (Proverbs 25:11).

Where is God when I've hurt my sister by saying something unkind? How can I change the way I speak to her?
Pleasant words are like a honeycomb, sweetness to the soul and health to the bones (Proverbs 16:24).

Where is God when I want to please Him by watching what I say to my family?
Let the words of my mouth and the meditation of my heart be acceptable in Your sight, O LORD, my strength and my Redeemer (Psalm 19:14).

Where is God when my brother is always blaming me for things he did?

All day they twist my words; all their thoughts are against me for evil (Psalm 56:5).

Where is God when I'm trying to learn how to communicate calmly instead of yelling?
Words of the wise, spoken quietly, should be heard rather than the shout of a ruler of fools (Ecclesiastes 9:17).

Growing Pains

(Family Struggles)

Pain amazes me with its crippling force and destructive energy. It doesn't take too long in working with young people to discover that pain is a regular part of their lives. Not every student comes from an unhealthy family, but many do. Alcoholic parents. Abusive parents. Parents who mortgage their kids for their jobs. Divorce. Affairs. The list goes on and on. Parents in pain. Kids in pain. Whole families in pain. How can destructive family pain be turned into a healthy type of growing pain?

Growing pains are a lot easier to deal with than family pains. Growing pains go away. Family pains tend to stick around longer. Sitting in a warm tub of water won't ease your family pains, but by His spirit, God can bring miraculous comfort and healing to your family. This stretching, pulling, ripping time you're going through now won't last forever. Even if you can't understand why God has allowed certain things to happen in your family, understand that God is with you in your pain.

Where is God when I wonder if He understands how unhealthy my family situation really is?
I will be glad and rejoice in Your mercy, for You have considered my trouble; You have known my soul in adversities (Psalm 31:7).

Where is God when I need to know that I can count on God to help me with my family problems?
Then they cried out to the LORD in their trouble, and He saved them out of their distresses (Psalm 107:19).

Where is God when I wonder if the pain in my family will ever end?
And God will wipe away every tear from their eyes; there shall be no more death, nor sorrow, nor crying. There shall be no more pain, for the former things have passed away (Revelation 21:4).

Where is God when my family problems affect everything I do and am?
For You have delivered my soul from death, my eyes from tears, and my feet from falling (Psalm 116:8).

Where is God when my parents don't understand me? Is God like my parents?
Gracious is the LORD, and righteous; yes, our God is merciful (Psalm 116:5).

Where is God when my parents don't seem to love me? Can God love me and care for me even though my parents don't?
He will feed His flock like a shepherd; He will gather the lambs with His arm, and carry them in His bosom, and gently lead those who are with young (Isaiah 40:11).

Where is God when all of my friends come from healthy homes and can't relate to my family problems?
I will be glad and rejoice in Your mercy, for You have considered my trouble; You have known my soul in adversities (Psalm 31:7).

Where is God when my friend's dad beats her? What can God do to help her?
I will deliver you from the hand of the wicked, and I will redeem you from the grip of the terrible (Jeremiah 15:21).

Where is God when I think about my family life and all I can do is cry?

Those who sow in tears shall reap in joy (Psalm 126:5).

Jell-O Through a Straw

(Family Living)

When was the last time you shook a bowl of Jell-O filled with minimarshmallows? Shake any part of the bowl and every single marshmallow in the goo will wobble. That's what a family is like. Whenever one part moves, the whole thing moves. Some people call it a family system. I call it Jell-O. Every person in the family is interrelated, interconnected, interimportant, and interdependent. It doesn't matter if you're mom, dad, sister, brother, adopted, step, or pet. Each person affects everyone else. No action or decision is made without having an impact on the whole bowl, er, family. Wobble, wobble.

Your decisions affect your whole family. That's why God places such importance on being obedient, listening to parents, having good attitudes, and being a contributor. Ignoring what your folks ask you to do. Mouthing off. Do these things and life in your family will definitely not gel. God's Word doesn't tell you to obey your parents for blind obedience' sake. He says it because obedience pleases Him. If you really want to please God, be willing to obey your parents.

Trying to do your own thing in your family while trying to live for God just won't work. It'll be as difficult as sucking Jell-O through a straw.

Where is God when I ignore what my parents have to say?
Listen to your father who begot you, and do not despise your mother when she is old (Proverbs 23:22).

Where is God when I want to know what the Bible says about having a good relationship with my dad?

The father of the righteous will greatly rejoice, and he who begets a wise child will delight in him (Proverbs 23:24).

Where is God when my parents drive me crazy by saying, "We told you so . . ."?
The way of a fool is right in his own eyes, but he who heeds counsel is wise (Proverbs 12:15).

Where is God when my parents, brothers, and sisters won't listen to me?
Hear my prayer, O LORD, give ear to my supplications! In Your faithfulness answer me, and in Your righteousness (Psalm 143:1).

Where is God when I know the Bible tells kids to obey their parents, but I want to know why?
Listen to counsel and receive instruction, that you may be wise in your latter days (Proverbs 19:20).

Where is God when my parents tell me I'm a great talker but a lousy listener?
He who answers a matter before he hears it, it is folly and shame to him (Proverbs 18:13).

Where is God when my parents tell me that I'm responsible for my own choices?
Cease listening to instruction, my son, and you will stray from the words of knowledge (Proverbs 19:27).

Where is God when I hate that my parents are always right?
Like an earring of gold and an ornament of fine gold is a wise rebuker to an obedient ear (Proverbs 25:12).

Where is God when my brother and I get in fights all the time?
A wrathful man stirs up strife, but he who is slow to anger allays contention (Proverbs 15:18).

Where is God when I'm quick to explode my anger toward my brothers and sisters?
Do not hasten in your spirit to be angry, for anger rests in the bosom of fools (Ecclesiastes 7:9).

Lying Through Your Teeth

(Lies)

Parents want to know the truth. You know how it goes: *the whole truth and nothing but the truth*. Students who struggle with lying to their parents never seem to figure out that truth builds exactly what they're looking for: trust. Trust is based upon telling the truth. I don't know how many times I've heard students say, "But my parents don't trust me, and they never will." Have you given them any reason to trust you?

God's Word talks a lot about honesty and integrity. Telling the truth to your parents may not win brownie points with your friends, but it may develop the trust that is critical to healthy relationships. Truth telling produces trust.

Where is God when I know I should be honest with my folks, but lying seems easier than telling the truth?
Remove from me the way of lying, and grant me Your law graciously. I have chosen the way of truth; Your judgments I have laid before me (Psalm 119:29–30).

Where is God when I smashed the car bumper and I'm tempted to lie about it?
Deliver my soul, O LORD, from lying lips and from a deceitful tongue (Psalm 120:2).

Where is God when I didn't realize that lying to my mom would hurt her so bad?
A wholesome tongue is a tree of life, but perverseness in it breaks the spirit (Proverbs 15:4).

Where is God when I got caught after sneaking out of the house and lying about it?
He who has a deceitful heart finds no good, and he who has a perverse tongue falls into evil (Proverbs 17:20).

Where is God when I wonder why it's so easy for me to distort the truth?
The heart is deceitful above all things, and desperately wicked; who can know it? (Jeremiah 17:9).

Where is God when other people in our neighborhood don't trust me because I've built a reputation for being a liar?
Therefore, putting away lying, "Let each one of you speak truth with his neighbor," for we are members of one another (Ephesians 4:25).

Where is God when I wonder about the benefits of honesty?
For "He who would love life and see good days, let him refrain his tongue from evil, and his lips from speaking deceit" (1 Peter 3:10).

Where is God when my brother is doing things I know he's not supposed to do? If my parents ask me, what should I tell them?
These are the things you shall do: speak each man the truth to his neighbor (Zechariah 8:16).

Where is God when I've been forging notes at school since I was a freshman and I haven't been caught yet?
A false witness will not go unpunished, and he who speaks lies shall perish (Proverbs 19:9).

Where is God when my parents caught me lying to them? I know lying hurts them, but how can it really hurt me?
Let no one deceive himself. If anyone among you seems to be wise in this age, let him become a fool that he may become wise (1 Corinthians 3:18).

Man Against Monster

(Sibling Rivalry)

I remember the day my brother Neil almost met his Maker. When we were kids, we spent Saturday afternoons watching cheesy old karate movies. You know, the Academy Award–winning movies that are famous for the sound coming two seconds after the actor's lips move. One day, Neil and I were out in front of the house, and he somehow thought he was Bruce Lee. We were goofing around, and he launched a fake karate kick into my face. The only problem was that his shoe didn't stay on his foot. *His shoe rocketed off and hit me in the mouth!* Joey O'Connor became Godzilla. Have you ever seen a Bruce Lee versus Godzilla movie? Man against monster is a rather ugly sight. Years have passed since that last altercation, and Neil's recovery has been slow but steady. Although he now walks with a slight limp, he's fortunate to be able to kick off his shoes.

Sibling rivalry has been around a long time. Cain took things a bit too far when he terminated his brother Abel. David's brothers laughed at him when he wanted to take on Goliath. Joseph, the dream boy, got pounded and thrown into an empty well for wearing color-coordinated clothes. His taste for high fashion did not impress his brothers. Sibling rivalry is part of growing up, and if you have brothers and sisters, you know what I mean. Even though there are always going to be fights, disagreements, shouting matches, and hurt feelings, God wants you to work out your problem so hurt doesn't turn into hatred. God is serious about loving the brothers and sisters He has given us. Don't let flying shoes karate chop your relationship in two.

Where is God when my brother constantly picks on me?
Repay no one evil for evil. Have regard for good things in the sight of all men (Romans 12:17).

Where is God when my sister spends hours in the bathroom?
Be kindly affectionate to one another with brotherly love, in honor giving preference to one another (Romans 12:10).

Where is God when my older brother gets all the attention because he's a great athlete and I'm not?
Therefore the LORD will wait, that He may be gracious to you; and therefore He will be exalted, that He may have mercy on you. For

the LORD is a God of justice; blessed are all those who wait for Him (Isaiah 30:18).

Where is God when I always get blamed for doing things that my sister does?
Therefore let us pursue the things which make for peace and the things by which one may edify another (Romans 14:19).

Where is God when my older brother is a total loser and I don't know how to help him?
If any of you lacks wisdom, let him ask of God, who gives to all liberally and without reproach, and it will be given to him (James 1:5).

Where is God when my sister says I'm a selfish pig?
Let no one seek his own, but each one the other's well-being (1 Corinthians 10:24).

Where is God when my mom just had a baby and I'm jealous that nobody pays attention to me anymore?
Cast your burden on the LORD, and He shall sustain you; He shall never permit the righteous to be moved (Psalm 55:22).

Where is God when my sister is always taking my clothes without asking?
And let us not grow weary while doing good, for in due season we shall reap if we do not lose heart (Galatians 6:9).

Where is God when I get into a fight with my brother, but I'm the one who gets punished?
If it is possible, as much as depends on you, live peaceably with all men (Romans 12:18).

Nobody Loves Me

(Feeling Unloved)

Have you ever wondered if the thought crossed Jesus' mind, *Does anybody love Me?* At one time, Jesus had thousands of followers, but He was down to just twelve. Lousy stats. Sure, He could whip up a fish and bread bash in a flash, but getting the crowds to stay for dessert was tough. He just couldn't hang on to His followers. Did He wonder if anybody really loved Him? Did the crowds even hear what He had to say about His Father's love? Would they ever get it? *Nobody loves Me.*

If you've ever felt as if nobody loves you, you and Jesus have a lot in common. Jesus knew He was hated. People wanted to drop-kick Him off a cliff. The crowds picked up rocks to play target practice with His brain. The religious leaders schemed. They plotted. They drew up a death plan. Jesus knew what it was like to feel unloved. That's why He chose to go to the cross. He wanted to prove His love for you so you would know that you are loved: "But God demonstrates His own love toward us, in that while we were still sinners, Christ died for us" (Romans 5:8). Next time you're feeling unloved, spend some time with Jesus. Tell Him whatever's on your mind. He's listening. You've got His complete attention. He knows how you feel.

Where is God when I have no one to talk to at home?
I pour out my complaint before Him; I declare before Him my trouble (Psalm 142:2).

Where is God when my family ignores my problems?
Casting all your care upon Him, for He cares for you (1 Peter 5:7).

Where is God when I was abandoned by my parents as a child and I know I'll never be able to speak with them?
When my father and my mother forsake me, then the LORD will take care of me (Psalm 27:10).

Where is God when I'm home alone after school and I'm afraid?
Be strong and of good courage, do not fear nor be afraid of them; for the LORD your God, He is the One who goes with you. He will not leave you nor forsake you (Deuteronomy 31:6).

Where is God when I can't handle the stress in my home?

In the multitude of my anxieties within me, Your comforts delight my soul (Psalm 94:19).

Where is God when my parents never do anything to my brother for beating me up?
"Do not be afraid of their faces, for I am with you to deliver you," says the LORD (Jeremiah 1:8).

Where is God when I need to be comforted and loved in a way that my family isn't capable of?
Sing, O heavens! Be joyful, O earth! And break out in singing, O mountains! For the LORD has comforted His people, and will have mercy on His afflicted (Isaiah 49:13).

Where is God when nobody at home cares about the others or talks about stuff that matters?
As one whom his mother comforts, so I will comfort you; and you shall be comforted in Jerusalem (Isaiah 66:13).

Where is God when my friend has the best parents in the world and I don't?
I know how to be abased, and I know how to abound. Everywhere and in all things I have learned both to be full and to be hungry, both to abound and to suffer need. I can do all things through Christ who strengthens me (Philippians 4:12–13).

Refrigerator Faith

(God Provides)

When I was growing up, my family had two refrigerators, one right next to the other. No, we weren't pigs, weight lifters, or grocers. When there are nine people in the family, you need two refrigerators or one large, restaurant-style refrigerator. My parents probably feared that I'd lock my sisters in the walk-in model, so they opted for two smaller, sister-safe refrigerators instead. We always had food on the table, clothes in the closets, and a roof over our heads. The food was good, the clothes fit, and when my sister was a baby, my dad found her strolling around naked on our two-story roof. That's another story, but all in all, my parents were good providers.

You may be able to relate to having your needs met as I experienced. I hope that's true. However, you may come from a home where money is a constant source of frustration and irritation. The recent struggles in our economy may have left your mom or dad without a job. Firings, layoffs, bankruptcy, bad business deals, and poor decision making can tear families apart quicker than you can say, "ATM."

You and your family matter to God. You are valuable to Him. If your family is having financial problems, focus your fears on your Provider. He promises to take care of you. He has a world full of resources. His refrigerator is a lot bigger than His bird feeder.

Where is God when my dad won't get a job? My mom works two jobs just to make ends meet!

But if anyone does not provide for his own, and especially for those of his household, he has denied the faith and is worse than an unbeliever (1 Timothy 5:8).

Where is God when my parents keep telling me I need to get a job to learn discipline with time, money, and work?

And let our people also learn to maintain good works, to meet urgent needs, that they may not be unfruitful (Titus 3:14).

Where is God when my brother asks to borrow ten bucks? Why should I lend it to him?

But you shall open your hand wide to him and willingly lend him sufficient for his need, whatever he needs (Deuteronomy 15:8).

Where is God when my parents make me help low-income people? Why is that our job?

If you extend your soul to the hungry and satisfy the afflicted soul, then your light shall dawn in the darkness, and your darkness shall be as the noonday (Isaiah 58:10).

Where is God when my family used to be rich, but now we have nothing?
For you know the grace of our Lord Jesus Christ, that though He was rich, yet for your sakes He became poor, that you through His poverty might become rich (2 Corinthians 8:9).

Where is God when my parents are always giving to charities?
Freely you have received, freely give (Matthew 10:8).

Where is God when my dad lost his job?
And my God shall supply all your need according to His riches in glory by Christ Jesus (Philippians 4:19).

Where is God when my parents tell me they can't afford to buy me the new clothes I need?
Therefore I say to you, do not worry about your life, what you will eat or what you will drink; nor about your body, what you will put on. Is not life more than food and the body more than clothing? (Matthew 6:25).

Where is God when I wonder if He cares about the money problems in my family?
I have learned in whatever state I am, to be content (Philippians 4:11).

Where is God when I worry about whether we'll be able to pay our rent at the end of the month?
Therefore do not worry about tomorrow, for tomorrow will worry about its own things. Sufficient for the day is its own trouble (Matthew 6:34).

Chapter SEVEN

School Survival

MY SCHOOL YEARS weren't easy for me. In the short span of six years, I attended five schools—two private and three public ones. That means I was a new kid five times. I hated being a new kid. The only school I didn't attend during junior high and high school was military school. I deserve a medal. Five of 'em. I'm a school survivor.

If you've hopped from school to school or if you're just trying to survive school one day at a time, we've got a lot in common. The funny thing is, my dad wasn't in the military, and his company didn't ship him all over the western United States. *We only moved once!* How I went to five schools in six years, I'm still trying to figure out. Here's the abbreviated version of my school survival history guide (I've left out the gory details for those of you with weak stomachs):

- *Fifth grade.* Valentine Elementary. A happy, unassuming little kid. An idyllic life. Little did I know what lay ahead.
- *Sixth and seventh grades.* We moved. My first private school. Fear. Weird uniforms. New kids. Made a touchdown. Made friends.
- *Eighth grade.* Niguel Hills Junior High. New school. Big place. Got lost first day of school. Almost cried trying to find classroom. Cool year. Skateboard team. Made lots of friends. First kiss. Wow!
- *Freshman year.* Resentencing. What did I do? Another prison, er, private school. Daily relocation. A forty-five-minute drive.

Weirder uniforms. Few friends. Complained all year long. (Ask my folks.)

- *Sophomore year*. Begged. Pleaded. Made runaway threats. Parents relented. Another new school. My choice. Parole granted upon good behavior. Free at last, free at last. Graduation 1982.

Surviving school can be the toughest thing you face as a teenager. But school isn't just about survival; it can be a positive experience. It's a place to meet new friends, share memories with old ones, and do all sorts of things you never got to do before. Clubs, sports teams, activities, and adventures are waiting to be experienced. Some students I know absolutely love school. Others can't stand it. They're sick of the cliques. The popularity game. The competition. The masks people wear trying to be someone they're not. They hate the pressure to use drugs and alcohol. Their friends tell them that if they're not sexually active, they must have a problem. For them, school isn't an education. It's a daily punishment for something they didn't do.

Whatever your experience with school has been so far, God wants you to know that He cares about you. He also cares about your school. He doesn't want you to be a mere survivor. He's concerned about you every morning when you wake up and head out the door to school. He cares about your friends, your homework, your pressures, and your questions about your future. He wants to be involved in your life. When you feel swatted down, He wants to pick you up. When you're excited about getting a good grade, He's ready to slap you a high-five. If you're lonely after a fight with a friend, He's the friend you need most.

Ambassador for Jesus

(Being Like Jesus)

What if you were sent to Somalia as a United Nations ambassador? What if it was your responsibility to help the millions of starving people in that war-torn country? Would you go?

You don't have to go to Somalia or India or South America to do something radical for Jesus. You don't have to wait for God to sky-write a message across the wild blue yonder to tell you what to do for Him. You can go right to your campus where students are starving for friendship. Desperate for someone who cares. You can do something radical for God today.

If you're a Christian, you're an official representative of Jesus Christ. You represent His love, His interests, and His concern for every person who doesn't know Him. *Does God expect me to take on my whole school?* No. The way to be an ambassador for Jesus is to make a difference for Him one person at a time.

Where is God when I want to help a girl who's got a lot of problems, but I don't know how?

I have shown you in every way, by laboring like this, that you must support the weak. And remember the words of the Lord Jesus, that He said, "It is more blessed to give than to receive" (Acts 20:35).

Where is God when I need courage to talk to a guy in my P.E. class about Christ?

And for me, that utterance may be given to me, that I may open my mouth boldly to make known the mystery of the gospel (Ephesians 6:19).

Where is God when I want to be a witness for Jesus on my campus?

Now then, we are ambassadors for Christ, as though God were pleading through us: we implore you on Christ's behalf, be reconciled to God (2 Corinthians 5:20).

Where is God when I'm sometimes scared to admit I'm a Christian?

For which I am an ambassador in chains; that in it I may speak boldly, as I ought to speak (Ephesians 6:20).

Where is God when I need His help not to fear what others think of me as a Christian?

For I am not ashamed of the gospel of Christ, for it is the power of God to salvation for everyone who believes, for the Jew first and also for the Greek (Romans 1:16).

Where is God when I recently became a Christian and now I get hassled all the time?

For this reason I also suffer these things; nevertheless I am not ashamed, for I know whom I have believed and am persuaded that He is able to keep what I have committed to Him until that Day (2 Timothy 1:12).

Where is God when my friends always pick on a freshman?

Defend the poor and fatherless; do justice to the afflicted and needy. Deliver the poor and needy; free them from the hand of the wicked (Psalm 82:3-4).

Where is God when I wonder if I should try to get to know the unpopular people at my school?

Better to be of a humble spirit with the lowly, than to divide the spoil with the proud (Proverbs 16:19).

Where is God when I want to know how I should make a difference on my campus?

The Spirit of the Lord is upon Me, because He has anointed Me to preach the gospel to the poor; He has sent Me to heal the broken-hearted, to proclaim liberty to the captives and recovery of sight to the blind, to set at liberty those who are oppressed (Luke 4:18).

Be a Difference Maker

(Changing Your World)

You want a simple way to be a difference maker? Here's a great idea that worked for us. Our youth ministry needed money to help students take trips. Many of our students had friends who couldn't afford the cost of camp. At the same time, we wanted to serve our community by doing the dirty work no one else wanted to do. A friend of mine in the Midwest told me how to raise scholarship money *and* serve the community.

Students raised money from family and friends for a one-day work project we called Project Serve. Instead of surfing, shopping at the mall, riding mountain bikes, or working out at the gym, about fifty students set out in teams to work their tails off for a whole day. One group cut a nature trail. Another group yanked weeds in a dirt lot the size of two football fields. Other teams painted a YMCA, planted flowers, and picked up trash in local parks and at Dana Point harbor. They were tired, sunburned, and worn out at the end of the day; the swimming pool was the only thing they didn't have to clean. Instead of expecting to be served all the time, the students learned to make a difference through serving.

Where is God when I don't seem to be making much of a difference as a Christian on the student council?

Therefore, my beloved brethren, be steadfast, immovable, always abounding in the work of the Lord, knowing that your labor is not in vain in the Lord (1 Corinthians 15:58).

Where is God when my Christian friends and I want to stand out for Christ on our campus? How can we do that?

By this all will know that you are My disciples, if you have love for one another (John 13:35).

Where is God when so many people at school try to bring attention to themselves?

Yet it shall not be so among you; but whoever desires to become great among you, let him be your servant (Matthew 20:26).

Where is God when I want to be like Christ among my friends, but I'm not sure how?

But he who is greatest among you shall be your servant. And whoever exalts himself will be humbled, and he who humbles himself will be exalted (Matthew 23:11–12).

Where is God when I've got all sorts of plans for things I want to do at school for Him?
His lord said to him, "Well done, good and faithful servant; you have been faithful over a few things, I will make you ruler over many things. Enter into the joy of your lord" (Matthew 25:23).

Where is God when I want to be completely open to God's will for my life?
Then Mary said, "Behold the maidservant of the Lord! Let it be to me according to your word" (Luke 1:38).

Where is God when I'm a leader on my campus, but I want to know how I can be a servant too?
If anyone serves Me, let him follow Me; and where I am, there My servant will be also. If anyone serves Me, him My Father will honor (John 12:26).

Where is God when I want to take my friendship with Jesus to school? Does Jesus consider me His friend?
No longer do I call you servants . . . but I have called you friends (John 15:15).

Where is God when I want to know how I can pray for my Christian friends at school?
That you may walk worthy of the Lord, fully pleasing Him, being fruitful in every good work and increasing in the knowledge of God (Colossians 1:10).

Cheating Yourself

(Cheating)

I can tell you how not to cheat. If you're going to cheat in your Spanish class, don't be stupid like I was. When I was in eighth grade, I thought I was a smart cheater. Wrong. If you're going to cheat, you need to remember three things: (1) never, I mean, never write your vocabulary words on your hand; (2) never cup your hand in front of your paper, stare at it, and then write the answer on your paper; and (3) never turn in your test with the same hand that has the answers on it. I know what you're wondering: *Is this guy lame or what?*

When the test was over, my teacher asked me to stay after class. Busted! She didn't have to say much. The evidence was written all over my face. And my hand. Did I learn my lesson? No. I kept cheating for the next couple of years until I finally slapped myself upside the head and asked myself, What am I doing? I may be getting a better grade, but I've also got this empty feeling inside.

You've heard it before: Cheaters never prosper. The only person you're cheating is yourself. Until you figure that out for yourself, you'll never understand. What more can I say? Don't write answers on your hand?

Where is God when I didn't study for a test, and the only way I'll pass this class is to cheat?
He who walks with integrity walks securely, but he who perverts his ways will become known (Proverbs 10:9).

Where is God when I can't stand the guy next to me who tries to cheat off my tests?
Rest in the LORD, and wait patiently for Him; do not fret because of him who prospers in his way, because of the man who brings wicked schemes to pass (Psalm 37:7).

Where is God when a few people sit around me who cheat on every test, and I'm afraid that I'll get blamed for cheating, too?
For I, the LORD your God, will hold your right hand, saying to you, "Fear not, I will help you" (Isaiah 41:13).

Where is God when I'm not a very good student, so the temptation to cheat is very strong?
Remove from me the way of lying, and grant me Your law graciously (Psalm 119:29).

Where is God when the girl next to me got caught for cheating and she accused me of helping her?
Deliver my soul, O LORD, from lying lips and from a deceitful tongue (Psalm 120:2).

Where is God when I keep telling my friend that he's going to get nailed for cheating, but he won't listen to me?
He who has a deceitful heart finds no good, and he who has a perverse tongue falls into evil (Proverbs 17:20).

Where is God when I wonder what harm there is in cheating?
For "He who would love life and see good days, let him refrain his tongue from evil, and his lips from speaking deceit" (1 Peter 3:10).

Where is God when I need to know what I can do to avoid the temptation of cheating?
LORD, who may abide in Your tabernacle? Who may dwell in Your holy hill? He who walks uprightly, and works righteousness, and speaks the truth in his heart (Psalm 15:1–2).

Where is God when my friend asked me to help him cheat?
These are the things you shall do: speak each man the truth to his neighbor (Zechariah 8:16).

Where is God when others make fun of me because I won't help others cheat on tests?
Listen to Me, you who know righteousness, you people in whose heart is My law: do not fear the reproach of men, nor be afraid of their insults (Isaiah 51:7).

Doing Unto Others

(This One's Tough)

Tom graduated from our high-school ministry a few years ago. He doesn't know it, but I used to brag about him all the time. People would ask about the ministry, and I'd tell 'em about Tom.

I asked Tom what he did during lunch at school. He told me that two or three times a week he would look for someone having lunch alone. He would go up to the person and ask if he could sit down. One time he had lunch with a boy who had just moved into the area. Another time he had lunch with a girl who had no friends. I wish I knew ten students with the guts to do what Tom did. Ten students who want to turn their world upside down for God. In God's eyes, Tom has class, pure class.

Where is God when I want to know how Jesus wants me to treat people at school?

Therefore, whatever you want men to do to you, do also to them, for this is the Law and the Prophets (Matthew 7:12).

Where is God when some friends are easily intimidated by other students?

Now we exhort you, brethren, warn those who are unruly, comfort the fainthearted, uphold the weak, be patient with all (1 Thessalonians 5:14).

Where is God when I want to be more consistent in making good decisions at school?

But let your "Yes" be "Yes," and your "No," "No" (Matthew 5:37).

Where is God when I have a friend who's always asking to borrow things, but I'm pretty selfish?

Give to him who asks you, and from him who wants to borrow from you do not turn away (Matthew 5:42).

Where is God when this guy at school constantly teases me and I can't stand it?

You have heard that it was said, "You shall love your neighbor and hate your enemy" (Matthew 5:43).

Where is God when my friends at school are pretty skeptical about Christianity?

Since you have purified your souls in obeying the truth through the Spirit in sincere love of the brethren, love one another fervently with a pure heart (1 Peter 1:22).

Where is God when everyone at school has an idea of what love is? How can I show people what God's love is?
By this we know love, because He laid down His life for us. And we also ought to lay down our lives for the brethren (1 John 3:16).

Where is God when people don't accept others at my school?
Therefore receive one another, just as Christ also received us, to the glory of God (Romans 15:7).

Where is God when I get tired of trying to live up to my reputation as a Christian?
And let us not grow weary while doing good, for in due season we shall reap if we do not lose heart (Galatians 6:9).

Running with a Gang

"He who is not with Me is against Me." If you're in a gang or you have friends who are, that's the type of language you understand. Either you're in the gang, or you're not. It's all or nothing. You can't live for Jesus and be in a gang. Jesus asks for total commitment. Just as the gang asks for your complete allegiance, Jesus is asking you to be totally sold out for Him.

If you're in a gang and have made a commitment to Christ, you need to make a decision. If you're thinking about joining a gang, slow down and think again. Joining a gang may get you all sorts of things you can't get on your own: protection, money, prestige, power. But what's the cost going to be?

Where is God when I want to stop gang violence on my campus, but I need His help?
Blessed are the peacemakers, for they shall be called sons of God (Matthew 5:9).

Where is God when I have a friend at school who's been telling me about Jesus, but I don't know if I'm ready yet? How can I know God's got something better for me?

But as it is written: "Eye has not seen, nor ear heard, nor have entered into the heart of man the things which God has prepared for those who love Him" (1 Corinthians 2:9).

Where is God when a friend at school is trying to get out of his gang, but he is afraid to do it? How can I help him?

Let him turn away from evil and do good; let him seek peace and pursue it (1 Peter 3:11).

Where is God when I'm going to get beaten by my gang for becoming a Christian?

But even if you should suffer for righteousness' sake, you are blessed. "And do not be afraid of their threats, nor be troubled" (1 Peter 3:14).

Where is God when I left my gang a few years ago and I think He's calling me to help others get out?

If I then, your Lord and Teacher, have washed your feet, you also ought to wash one another's feet. For I have given you an example, that you should do as I have done to you (John 13:14–15).

Where is God when there's a rumor that I'm going to get jumped by some gang members because I'm outspoken for Jesus?

Blessed are those who are persecuted for righteousness' sake, for theirs is the kingdom of heaven (Matthew 5:10).

Where is God when I don't know how it's possible for me to be a peacemaker on my campus?

If it is possible, as much as depends on you, live peaceably with all men (Romans 12:18).

Where is God when I'm afraid to lose my life for Jesus because my gang will make sure I do?

For whoever desires to save his life will lose it, but whoever loses his life for My sake will save it. For what profit is it to a man if he gains the whole world, and is himself destroyed or lost? (Luke 9:24–25).

Where is God when a group of girls taunt me because I won't join their gang?
Blessed are you when they revile and persecute you, and say all kinds of evil against you falsely for My sake. Rejoice and be exceedingly glad, for great is your reward in heaven, for so they persecuted the prophets who were before you (Matthew 5:11–12).

Where is God when I want to get out of my gang, but I'm afraid to take a stand for Jesus?
For whoever is ashamed of Me and My words, of him the Son of Man will be ashamed when He comes in His own glory, and in His Father's, and of the holy angels (Luke 9:26).

Hanging Out with Jesus

(Friendship with God)

Jesus hung out with a group of twelve guys a couple of thousand years ago. But who does Jesus get to hang out with now? If Jesus were sitting at one of the lunch tables at your school, would you have lunch with Him?

If He were a new kid on campus who just moved from Alaska, would you invite Him to hang out with your friends? What if He were the last one to be picked when choosing sides for basketball? Would you pick Him? A poor carpenter's son from out of town?

Where is God when hanging out with Jesus may mean losing some of my friends?
Then He said to them all, "If anyone desires to come after Me, let him deny himself, and take up his cross daily, and follow Me" (Luke 9:23).

Where is God when I want to know how Jesus had time for His Father in the midst of His busy schedule?

Now in the morning, having risen a long while before daylight, He went out and departed to a solitary place; and there He prayed (Mark 1:35).

Where is God when my life is surrounded by people? How can I get to know Jesus better if I'm always with people?

And when He had sent the multitudes away, He went up on the mountain by Himself to pray. Now when evening came, He was alone there (Matthew 14:23).

Where is God when I want my friends at school to know I'm a Christian, but I'm an easy target for temptation?

Watch and pray, lest you enter into temptation. The spirit indeed is willing, but the flesh is weak (Matthew 26:41).

Where is God when I want to learn how to know Jesus better?

Pray without ceasing (1 Thessalonians 5:17).

Where is God when I am torn between spending time with Jesus and spending time with my friends?

I am the vine, you are the branches. He who abides in Me, and I in him, bears much fruit; for without Me you can do nothing (John 15:5).

Where is God when I need to know how to keep a solid friendship with Him?

As the Father loved Me, I also have loved you; abide in My love (John 15:9).

Where is God when it seems so easy to get swayed away from Christ?

If you keep My commandments, you will abide in My love, just as I have kept My Father's commandments and abide in His love (John 15:10).

Where is God when I want to tell my friends about my relationship with Jesus, but I'm not sure how?

Then He said to them, "Follow Me, and I will make you fishers of men" (Matthew 4:19).

Living Counterclockwise

(Thoughts and Attitudes)

Turn the dial counterclockwise two spins to 17, clockwise one whole spin to 34, then back again to 7, or was it 5 or 25? I always hated getting new locker combinations. At my school, they put your locker combination on a tiny piece of paper, expected you to memorize it before noon, and then swallow it like a spy. Spinning the locker dial back and forth in frustration, I looked real intelligent standing in the hallway all alone after the late bell rang. Smooth, real smooth.

Each day we get bombarded with endless messages, advertising, and pressures telling us how we're supposed to live. The world tells us to live clockwise, yet God's message to us is to live counterclockwise. Like lockers, our minds are meant to hold all sorts of information, the right kind of information. The Bible tells us to fill our minds with His Word so we won't be swayed back and forth by every new trend that comes our way. God wants us to remember who we are in Christ.

Where is God when I want to know how to love Him with my mind?
Jesus said to him, "You shall love the LORD your God with all your heart, with all your soul, and with all your mind" (Matthew 22:37).

Where is God when I get so frustrated trying to think good thoughts, but all I think are bad ones?
I thank God—through Jesus Christ our Lord! So then, with the mind I myself serve the law of God, but with the flesh the law of sin (Romans 7:25).

Where is God when I want to get my mind under His control?
For to be carnally minded is death, but to be spiritually minded is life and peace. Because the carnal mind is enmity against God; for it is not subject to the law of God, nor indeed can be (Romans 8:6–7).

Where is God when my brain gets so caught up in society's values that I have a hard time understanding what's important to God?
And do not be conformed to this world, but be transformed by the renewing of your mind, that you may prove what is that good and acceptable and perfect will of God (Romans 12:2).

Where is God when a few of my conservative Christian friends differ from me on several important issues?
Therefore let us not judge one another anymore, but rather resolve this, not to put a stumbling block or a cause to fall in our brother's way (Romans 14:13).

Where is God when I can spend a whole day without even thinking about Him once?
Therefore, holy brethren, partakers of the heavenly calling, consider the Apostle and High Priest of our confession, Christ Jesus (Hebrews 3:1).

Where is God when my friends tell me I'm too sure of myself at times?
For I say, through the grace given to me, to everyone who is among you, not to think of himself more highly than he ought to think, but to think soberly, as God has dealt to each one a measure of faith (Romans 12:3).

Where is God when I'm really struggling with lust?
But put on the Lord Jesus Christ, and make no provision for the flesh, to fulfill its lusts (Romans 13:14).

Where is God when my Christian friends and I get into intellectual arguments to see who's smarter, but we always end up fighting?

Now I plead with you, brethren, by the name of our Lord Jesus Christ, that you all speak the same thing, and that there be no divisions among you, but that you be perfectly joined together in the same mind and in the same judgment (1 Corinthians 1:10).

Where is God when I've been doing really good lately by not giving in to impure thoughts, but want to keep my mind on track?
Therefore let him who thinks he stands take heed lest he fall (1 Corinthians 10:12).

Lousy Study Habits

(Self-Explanatory)

TV or trigonometry? "Monday Night Football" or music theory? Swirl your gum or study? Gym or geometry? Procrastinate or prepare for finals? Lousy study habits are a lot more than procrastination. They're a way of life.

Developing good study habits is harder than maintaining lousy ones. If you're a lousy student or a hopeless procrastinator, don't be too hard on yourself. If you're too hard on yourself, chances are, you'll just put off your homework even longer. Start where you are. Do what you can do now. If you need help, ask someone. God understands your situation. No matter what, He won't delay helping you.

Where is God when I wonder if anyone in the Bible can relate to having a ton of homework?
And I set my heart to seek and search out by wisdom concerning all that is done under heaven; this burdensome task God has given to the sons of man, by which they may be exercised (Ecclesiastes 1:13).

Where is God when I keep falling asleep while doing my homework?

And further, my son, be admonished by these. Of making many books there is no end, and much study is wearisome to the flesh (Ecclesiastes 12:12).

Where is God when my parents get on my case for not studying enough?
The fear of the LORD is the beginning of knowledge, but fools despise wisdom and instruction (Proverbs 1:7).

Where is God when my friends and I get together to study, but we never get anything done?
He who keeps instruction is in the way of life, but he who refuses correction goes astray (Proverbs 10:17).

Where is God when my grades are so bad that I need a tutor, but I don't like someone else telling me how to do things?
Whoever loves instruction loves knowledge, but he who hates correction is stupid (Proverbs 12:1)

Where is God when my lousy study habits make me feel bad about myself?
He who disdains instruction despises his own soul, but he who heeds rebuke gets understanding (Proverbs 15:32).

Where is God when I'm not a very good student because I never study and I make fun of others who do?
If you are wise, you are wise for yourself, and if you scoff, you will bear it alone (Proverbs 9:12).

Where is God when I'm trying really hard to do better in geometry, but I get easily discouraged?
If any of you lacks wisdom, let him ask of God, who gives to all liberally and without reproach, and it will be given to him (James 1:5).

Where is God when my teachers unload a huge pile of homework on me and I don't see how I can possibly hurdle it?
For by You I can run against a troop; by my God I can leap over a wall (2 Samuel 22:30).

Where is God when my classes are so frustrating, I get so upset I start crying? Does He hear my prayers for help?
Give heed to the voice of my cry, my King and my God, for to You I will pray (Psalm 5:2).

Where is God when I've blown off a lot of homework and I need His help to finish it all tonight?
Behold, God is my helper; the Lord is with those who uphold my life (Psalm 54:4).

No Talking, Please

(Talking in Class)

I get disappointed when I hear Christian students ripping on their teachers. *I can't stand Mr. So-and-So! He's the worst teacher in the whole world!* The worst teacher in the whole world? How can Christians praise God and curse people made in His image? The book of James talks about the power of the tongue and its destructive nature. Teachers are people with problems, feelings, struggles, and pressures just like you. Lighten up on 'em! Let your actions and words in class reveal *who* you know and not just *what* you know. Next time you're tempted to open your mouth with nothing to say, remember this: *En boca cerrada, no entran las moscas* (flies don't enter a closed mouth).

Where is God when my teacher thinks I'm obnoxious because I'm always talking?
The wise in heart will receive commands, but a prating fool will fall (Proverbs 10:8).

Where is God when I sit next to a girl who gossips all the time? She drives me crazy!
He who goes about as a talebearer reveals secrets; therefore do not associate with one who flatters with his lips (Proverbs 20:19).

Where is God when fights break out in my classes because people constantly rip on each other?
The mouth of the righteous is a well of life, but violence covers the mouth of the wicked (Proverbs 10:11).

Where is God when my teacher tells me that talking in class is hurting my grades?
Wise people store up knowledge, but the mouth of the foolish is near destruction (Proverbs 10:14).

Where is God when everyone in my class talks about each other, so I wonder what's wrong with a little gossip?
Whoever hides hatred has lying lips, and whoever spreads slander is a fool (Proverbs 10:18).

Where is God when my teacher always singles me out for talking?
In the multitude of words sin is not lacking, but he who restrains his lips is wise (Proverbs 10:19).

Where is God when this guy in my class says really crude things?
The lips of the righteous know what is acceptable, but the mouth of the wicked what is perverse (Proverbs 10:32).

Where is God when I know I'm not setting a very good example as a Christian by talking in class, but is there anything really wrong with it?
Therefore, to him who knows to do good and does not do it, to him it is sin (James 4:17).

Where is God when my teacher treats us like slaves?
Bondservants, be obedient to those who are your masters according to the flesh, with fear and trembling, in sincerity of heart, as to Christ (Ephesians 6:5).

Question Authority

(Authority Figures)

Don't tell me! Let me guess. Your vice principal is a slimy bald-headed power freak. Am I close? Let me try another. Your coach is into pain and power and takes pleasure in seeing young people bleed. Right? I thought so! Your parents? Controlling paranoid life forms wearing polyester. Did I hit the mark? Every person over twenty-two years old is out to get you. You can't figure out what you've done, but you know they're all against you, right? That's why you question authority. I thought so.

Questioning authority is OK if you're searching for truth. Questioning authority is OK if there's a clear abuse of authority. But questioning or challenging authority so you can get your own way is selfish. It's called manipulation. Many students have problems with authority because of poor relationships with their parents. And for an abused person, questioning authority is a means of protection and self-preservation. That's healthy. Questioning authority to avoid responsibility or to blame others doesn't count. If you can't accept authority from others, how will you ever learn to accept God's authority in your life? Question authority for truth's sake, not your own.

Where is God when the people in authority at my school make authority stink?
Obey those who rule over you, and be submissive, for they watch out for your souls, as those who must give account. Let them do so with joy and not with grief, for that would be unprofitable for you (Hebrews 13:17).

Where is God when it seems that every adult at my school wants to order me around?
Therefore submit yourselves to every ordinance of man for the Lord's sake (1 Peter 2:13).

Where is God when I can't understand why our school has the worst principal in the world?

Let every soul be subject to the governing authorities. For there is no authority except from God, and the authorities that exist are appointed by God (Romans 13:1).

Where is God when I want to know if it's OK to rebel against school rules that everyone thinks are wrong anyway?

Therefore whoever resists the authority resists the ordinance of God, and those who resist will bring judgment on themselves (Romans 13:2).

Where is God when I don't want to do what I'm told to do at school, but I feel guilty doing something wrong?

Therefore you must be subject, not only because of wrath but also for conscience' sake (Romans 13:5).

Where is God when I wonder if He expects me to respect a vice principal who's completely unrespectable?

Render therefore to all their due: taxes to whom taxes are due, customs to whom customs, fear to whom fear, honor to whom honor (Romans 13:7).

Where is God when I know it's right to listen to school authorities, but there's something inside me that can't wait to rebel?

Therefore submit to God. Resist the devil and he will flee from you (James 4:7).

Where is God when the vice principal at my school is an angry person? Even though I don't like him, what would God want me to do?

[Submit] to one another in the fear of God (Ephesians 5:21).

Where is God when I don't want to cause trouble at school, but I'm afraid my friends will bug me if I don't do the bad things they do? Will God watch out for me?

For the LORD knows the way of the righteous, but the way of the ungodly shall perish (Psalm 1:6).

Chapter EIGHT

Help Wanted

IT ALL STARTED with a stupid used yellow surfboard. I was in the fourth grade, and *I thought I wanted to learn how to surf.* Wanting to teach me a few lessons about the value of work and money management, my dad offered me a deal that got me a surfboard and him a gardener. The surfboard cost forty dollars. For one dollar an hour, I could pay off the surfboard by cleaning the front and back yards of our home every week. Mowing the lawn and hosing down the driveway got old fast, but I was stuck. Every week, cleaning the yard took only two hours, so after twenty weeks (five long months), I was eager for early retirement from the Garden Committee.

When we're young, work looks fun and exciting, but as we get older, many of us consider work exactly what it's called: a chore. But work doesn't have to be a chore if you understand its importance and its benefits. The most obvious reason for young people to work is money. Cash. Money enables you to buy the stuff you want and do the things you want to do. Young people work for many other reasons, however. Some teenagers have to work because their families have a low income, and their help is needed to pay bills. Some young people work to avoid spending time at home with a family that has serious problems. Some teenagers work because it gives them a sense of independence and responsibility that can build self-esteem. Whatever the reason for going out and getting a job as a teenager, having a job ultimately prepares you for what you will spend the rest of your life doing: WORKING!

The Bible is filled with ideas, thoughts, and principles about work and how to handle the money you earn from your job. God is interested in how you perform on your job, whether you are self-employed or employed in missile deployment. He is interested in your decisions concerning integrity, materialism, customers, honesty, conflicts with coworkers, bosses, money, and Uncle Sam's share of your *dinero*.

Who's the Boss?

(Working with Bosses)

Let's face one simple fact: When you work for someone else, your job is on the line. You report to your boss, whether an Attila the Hun out to make your work excruciatingly painful or a push-over. A boss's role is to hold you accountable to perform a specific task and to see that you do it well. It doesn't matter if you're plucking leaves and lizard guts out of lawnmower blades or balancing the federal budget, somewhere in the chain of command, somebody created your job because it serves a specific function. You're a Christian, and the way you perform your job speaks loudly about your faith.

Where is God when I feel like telling my boss what I really think of him?
Out of the same mouth proceed blessing and cursing. My brethren, these things ought not to be so (James 3:10).

Where is God when my boss is from another country and we have communication problems?
So then, my beloved brethren, let every man be swift to hear, slow to speak, slow to wrath (James 1:19).

Where is God when my boss schedules me to work the same day that I asked a girl out for a date? Should I call in sick?

Do not lie to one another, since you have put off the old man with his deeds (Colossians 3:9).

Where is God when my boss is a jerk?
But love your enemies, do good, and lend, hoping for nothing in return; and your reward will be great, and you will be sons of the Most High. For He is kind to the unthankful and evil (Luke 6:35).

Where is God when I'm angry with my boss for scheduling me to work weekends?
A fool vents all his feelings, but a wise man holds them back (Proverbs 29:11).

Where is God when my boss yells at me in front of other co-workers? I feel like getting even!
Beloved, do not avenge yourselves, but rather give place to wrath; for it is written, "Vengeance is Mine, I will repay," says the Lord (Romans 12:19).

Where is God when my boss asks me to do something unethical? I want to have integrity.
Far be it from me that I should say you are right; till I die I will not put away my integrity from me (Job 27:5).

Where is God when my boss is unfair and tends to play favorites?
The discretion of a man makes him slow to anger, and his glory is to overlook a transgression (Proverbs 19:11).

Where is God when I believe it is in our customers' best interests to inform the county health department about the kitchen at work, but I'm afraid of losing my job?
But even if you should suffer for righteousness' sake, you are blessed (1 Peter 3:14).

Where is God when my boss makes promises she doesn't keep? Does God ever break His promises?
And you know in all your hearts and in all your souls that not one thing has failed of all the good things which the LORD your God spoke concerning you (Joshua 23:14).

Where is God when my car broke down, which made me late for work, and my boss didn't believe me?
Likewise you younger people, submit yourselves to your elders. Yes, all of you be submissive to one another, and be clothed with humility, for "God resists the proud, but gives grace to the humble" (1 Peter 5:5).

Where is God when I work hard to get a raise, but the boss doesn't give me one?
The plans of the diligent lead surely to plenty, but those of everyone who is hasty, surely to poverty (Proverbs 21:5).

Where is God when I wonder if the only reason I work hard is to please the boss? Should I work hard to please God too?
I, the LORD, search the heart, I test the mind, even to give every man according to his ways, according to the fruit of his doings (Jeremiah 17:10).

Where is God when it doesn't seem to matter if I do a job well or not?
In all labor there is profit, but idle chatter leads only to poverty (Proverbs 14:23).

Where is God when my boss threatens to fire me for not working as I should?
And we urge you, brethren, to recognize those who labor among you, and are over you in the Lord and admonish you (1 Thessalonians 5:12).

Where is God when I'm accused of stealing, but I didn't do anything?
Righteousness guards him whose way is blameless, but wickedness overthrows the sinner (Proverbs 13:6).

Where is God when my boss works me harder than Genghis Khan would?
And whatever you do in word or deed, do all in the name of the Lord Jesus, giving thanks to God the Father through Him (Colossians 3:17).

Where is God when my job environment is very stressful?
Peace I leave with you, My peace I give to you; not as the world gives do I give to you. Let not your heart be troubled, neither let it be afraid (John 14:27).

Where is God when my boss calls me at home and tells me he wants to see me immediately? I don't think I did anything wrong, but I'm scared.
For I, the LORD your God, will hold your right hand, saying to you, "Fear not, I will help you" (Isaiah 41:13).

Where is God when nobody seems to notice how hard I work?
That you may walk worthy of the Lord, fully pleasing Him, being fruitful in every good work and increasing in the knowledge of God (Colossians 1:10).

Where is God when my boss forces me to work on Sundays? What can I tell him?
Remember the Sabbath day, to keep it holy (Exodus 20:8).

Living Beyond Minimum Wage

Working for minimum wage can be lousy. Having a minimum wage job means wiping the gooey sludge under dripping refrigerators, taking out tons of stinking trash, sweeping, painting, mopping, scrubbing, filling and emptying bins, and disinfecting every toilet, sink, trashcan, and countertop in sight. Grunt labor . . who needs it? Who wants it? But if you're short on cash and need a job, what else can you do?

If you're like most teenagers, you'd probably like the idea of being the president, CEO, boss, and owner of the company your very first day on the job. "Sorry, that position has already been filled, but we could use some help in the company Laundromat." The majority of jobs for young people pay minimum wage because most positions at that pay scale do not require any experience. Removing toxic waste requires more knowledge and experience than ripping tickets at the entrance of a movie theater. You may not get strange diseases from taking tickets, but you also won't make $100,000 a year.

However, if you want to earn more than minimum wage, the quickest way is to let your employer see a good attitude and your ability to be responsible with whatever job you've been given to do. In Jesus' words, be faithful in the little things before expecting the bigger and better glamour jobs.

Investing in Integrity

(Integrity)

Today many people have said *adios* to integrity instead of *sayonara* to selfishness. Integrity was once a hot item on the market in this country. Things like being honest, keeping your word, and being reliable were the crucial ingredients to secure trust in relationships. That leaves you with a dilemma: Are you going to invest in integrity or splurge on selfishness? Living God's way means *not* being dishonest, stealing out of the cash register, ripping off clothes from work, or cheating on your time card. Living God's way means making some tough choices because being selfish comes naturally. Investing in selfishness may have short-term payoffs, but they'll depreciate you as a person. Investing in integrity will not only help you learn how to honor God; it'll yield eternal dividends that can't be measured in dollars and cents.

Where is God when I'm tempted to steal merchandise?
God is faithful, who will not allow you to be tempted beyond what you are able, but with the temptation will also make the way of escape, that you may be able to bear it (1 Corinthians 10:13).

Where is God when I feel like skipping work? Would it matter just this once?

The backslider in heart will be filled with his own ways, but a good man will be satisfied from above (Proverbs 14:14).

Where is God when I don't see much integrity at work, so I wonder what difference can I make?
The integrity of the upright will guide them, but the perversity of the unfaithful will destroy them (Proverbs 11:3).

Where is God when I don't think teenagers should have to pay the IRS?
They said to Him, "Caesar's." And He said to them, "Render therefore to Caesar the things that are Caesar's, and to God the things that are God's" (Matthew 22:21).

Where is God when I'm asked to do things at work I don't want to do?
For even the Son of Man did not come to be served, but to serve, and to give His life a ransom for many (Mark 10:45).

Where is God when I feel like being lazy at work?
The soul of a lazy man desires, and has nothing; but the soul of the diligent shall be made rich (Proverbs 13:4).

Where is God when other people at work cut corners and I want to do the same?
Let integrity and uprightness preserve me, for I wait for You (Psalm 25:21).

Where is God when a friend at work steals and I don't know what to tell her?
Let him who stole steal no longer, but rather let him labor, working with his hands what is good (Ephesians 4:28).

Where is God when I'm sick and tired of doing other people's jobs?
He who is slow to anger is better than the mighty, and he who rules his spirit than he who takes a city (Proverbs 16:32).

Where is God when I'd rather hit the snooze button than go to work?

The hand of the diligent will rule, but the lazy man will be put to forced labor (Proverbs 12:24).

Where is God when I want to be a person of integrity, but with so much cash in the register, I'm tempted to steal it?
You shall not steal (Exodus 20:15).

Dealing with Cash

(Being Wise with $$$)

Would you believe that money is important to God? Did you know that the Bible talks about money more than it talks about love? I believe that God thinks money is important because it gets people's attention. Hold up a Brink's truck. Rob a bank. You'll get plenty of attention. A lot of people love money more than they do God. If money has more of your attention than God does or you're wondering how to use your cash in a way that pleases God, these verses will help you learn what God thinks about money.

Where is God when I'm having trouble saving money?
He who tills his land will have plenty of bread, but he who follows frivolity will have poverty enough! (Proverbs 28:19).

Where is God when my pay is low and I sometimes help myself to some merchandise?
Do not overwork to be rich; because of your own understanding, cease! Will you set your eyes on that which is not? For riches certainly make themselves wings; they fly away like an eagle toward heaven (Proverbs 23:4–5).

Where is God when I've borrowed money I can't pay back?
Go and humble yourself; plead with your friend (Proverbs 6:3).

Where is God when I'm not sure if I should financially support an orphan child in another country?

But whoever has this world's goods, and sees his brother in need, and shuts up his heart from him, how does the love of God abide in him? (1 John 3:17).

Where is God when I have trouble tithing my money?
So let each one give as he purposes in his heart, not grudgingly or of necessity; for God loves a cheerful giver (2 Corinthians 9:7).

Where is God when someone messes up on my paycheck and I don't get the money I deserve?
He who covers a transgression seeks love, but he who repeats a matter separates friends (Proverbs 17:9).

Where is God when I want to be wise with my money?
For wisdom is a defense as money is a defense, but the excellence of knowledge is that wisdom gives life to those who have it (Ecclesiastes 7:12).

When You Hate Your Coworkers

(Getting Along with Others)

Right now, you may be working with someone you can't stand. In fact, trouble, strife, conflict, wars, gossip, cruel pranks, anger, problems, jealousy, fits of rage, and hatred are quite common among people who work together. *But* just because you've thought of asking your boss for hazardous duty pay doesn't mean that you can't change the way you respond to problems at work. God's Word will teach you how to deal with problems, how to get along with people, and how to respond in difficult situations. Jesus Christ wants us to love our enemies as He loved His enemies. If you're going to hate, hate the things Jesus hates. Hate sin and hypocrisy, not people.

Where is God when I'm the only Christian at my job?

Let your light so shine before men, that they may see your good works and glorify your Father in heaven (Matthew 5:16).

Where is God when the people I work with are always telling gross jokes?
But shun profane and idle babblings, for they will increase to more ungodliness (2 Timothy 2:16).

Where is God when I work on commission and a coworker is always stealing my customers?
Brethren, if a man is overtaken in any trespass, you who are spiritual restore such a one in a spirit of gentleness, considering yourself lest you also be tempted (Galatians 6:1).

Where is God when I don't feel like being a Christian at work?
For you have need of endurance, so that after you have done the will of God, you may receive the promise (Hebrews 10:36).

Where is God when the people I work with are unbearable?
He who is slow to wrath has great understanding, but he who is impulsive exalts folly (Proverbs 14:29).

Where is God when the people I work with gossip all the time and I'm tempted to join them?
The words of a talebearer are like tasty trifles, and they go down into the inmost body (Proverbs 18:8).

Where is God when my friend makes little adjustments on her time card and tells me to do the same? What does God want me to do?
I know also, my God, that You test the heart and have pleasure in uprightness (1 Chronicles 29:17).

Where is God when no one has to clean the ashtrays but me?
He has cast me into the mire, and I have become like dust and ashes (Job 30:19).

Where is God when I have to work with incompetent people? I know I'm not better than anyone else, but what kind of attitude does God want me to have?

For you, brethren, have been called to liberty; only do not use liberty as an opportunity for the flesh, but through love serve one another (Galatians 5:13).

Where is God when I get caught lying for a coworker? What does God say about lying?
Lying lips are an abomination to the LORD, but those who deal truthfully are His delight (Proverbs 12:22).

Where is God when people at work never ask me to eat lunch with them?
Turn Yourself to me, and have mercy on me, for I am desolate and afflicted. The troubles of my heart have enlarged; bring me out of my distresses! (Psalm 25:16–17).

Fringe Benefit Friendships

(Using Your Friends)

In other languages and cultures, it's called stealing or theft. For a lot of teenagers in the U.S., it's called employee discount, or "Don't worry about it," or "Go now! My boss isn't looking!" It's what I call a fringe benefit friendship—your friends know that your job is their ticket to a free ride. That puts you in a difficult situation: Do you let your friends slide and give them anything they want, or do you choose to be a person of integrity and refuse to give in to their requests?

It's a crime to steal, no matter how small the scoop may be. Having friends steal for you is an even bigger crime. Stealing for friends cheapens friendship and devalues you as a person. Friends who want stuff and not a quality friendship are basically saying, "I don't care if you lose your job. I'm interested in stuff and not you." Don't live on the fringe.

Where is God when my friends ask me to buy them stuff with my employee discount and I know it's not right?

My son, if sinners entice you, do not consent. If they say, "Come with us, . . . We shall find all kinds of precious possessions, we shall fill our houses with spoil; cast in your lot among us, let us all have one purse"—My son, do not walk in the way with them, keep your foot from their path (Proverbs 1:10–11, 13–15).

Where is God when I work at a movie theater and my friends spend all day hopping from one movie to the next? Is it wrong for me to ignore this problem?
The way of the wicked is an abomination to the LORD, but He loves him who follows righteousness (Proverbs 15:9).

Where is God when I'm jealous because my friends get all the money they want from their folks and I have to work?
For where envy and self-seeking exist, confusion and every evil thing are there (James 3:16).

Where is God when all my friends have jobs that pay really well and I get only minimum wage?
He who loves silver will not be satisfied with silver; nor he who loves abundance, with increase. This also is vanity (Ecclesiastes 5:10).

Where is God when I work at an ice cream shop and my friends hassle me if I don't give them free cones?
He who loves silver will not be satisfied with silver; nor he who loves abundance, with increase. This also is vanity (Ecclesiastes 5:10).

Where is God when I drop a whole tray of dishes in front of a bunch of good-looking girls?
Let them be confounded because of their shame, who say to me, "Aha, aha!" (Psalm 40:15).

Where is God when my Christian friends are always so competitive about who makes more money?
Let them do good, that they be rich in good works, ready to give, willing to share (1 Timothy 6:18).

Where is God when my busy work schedule seriously hampers my social life?
But You, O LORD, do not be far from Me; O My Strength, hasten to help Me! (Psalm 22:19).

My Parents Made Me Get a Job

(Having to Work)

I'll never forget the day my dad took me down to Mac's Coffee Break when I was thirteen years old. "Are you hiring any dishwashers?" he asked. I was sarcastically thinking, *How did Dad know I'd rather wash dishes all summer instead of going to the beach?* That summer I peeled potatoes, mopped scum off a sticky floor, and bused trays filled with half-eaten French toast, runny eggs, ketchup-smeared plates, and terminated tuna salads. Working at Mac's was a drag. And I only worked two or three days a week.

If your parents want you to get a job, there's a good chance they're trying to teach you some essential lessons about money and responsibility. Is God the same way? No! He won't ever force you to wash Idaho potatoes or send you to Zaire to work with people who have no work or insist that you cut your hair when you want it long instead of short. But His Word contains ideas, principles, lessons, and truths about parent-enforced work that can teach you how to live life like it isn't a part-time job.

Where is God when I have to use my money to pay for my family's needs?
But if anyone does not provide for his own, and especially for those of his household, he has denied the faith and is worse than an unbeliever (1 Timothy 5:8).

Where is God when my parents expect me to get good grades and do well in sports, and now they're pressuring me to get a job?
For we do not want you to be ignorant, brethren, of our trouble

which came to us in Asia: that we were burdened beyond measure, above strength, so that we despaired even of life. Yes, we had the sentence of death in ourselves, that we should not trust in ourselves but in God who raises the dead (2 Corinthians 1:8–9).

Where is God when my parents say that if I want to go to college, I have to start saving money now?
Wealth gained by dishonesty will be diminished, but he who gathers by labor will increase (Proverbs 13:11).

Where is God when I really need a job, but I can't seem to get one? My parents don't believe me.
Commit your works to the LORD, and your thoughts will be established (Proverbs 16:3).

Where is God when I'm so tired after work that I don't have the strength or motivation to do my chores at home?
Seek the LORD and His strength; seek His face evermore! (Psalm 105:4).

Where is God when my parents promised my uncle—without first asking me—that I'd work for him? How can I tell my uncle I don't want to work for him?
For even your brothers, the house of your father, even they have dealt treacherously with you (Jeremiah 12:6).

Material Madness

(Materialism)

A major motivating factor for having a job is getting cash to buy stuff. You live in a society that prides itself on buying, owning, keeping, and hoarding stuff that God says will ultimately pass away. When you place too much importance on material things, you forget what's really vital in life. An insatiable desire to hold onto things that break, get old, or get lost is a waste of the precious time you have on this earth.

Where is God when I have to choose between buying a new stereo or going on the youth retreat?
Do not lay up for yourselves treasures on earth, . . . but lay up for yourselves treasures in heaven (Matthew 6:19–20).

Where is God when I feel secure by having a lot of material possessions?
Now godliness with contentment is great gain. For we brought nothing into this world, and it is certain we can carry nothing out (1 Timothy 6:6–7).

Where is God when all I want to do is to spend my money on material things?
Jesus said to him, "If you want to be perfect, go, sell what you have and give to the poor, and you will have treasure in heaven; and come, follow Me" (Matthew 19:21).

Where is God when I have a problem with overspending?
No one can serve two masters; for either he will hate the one and love the other, or else he will be loyal to the one and despise the other. You cannot serve God and mammon (Matthew 6:24).

Where is God when I can't help comparing myself to my friends who have so much stuff?
Therefore I say to you, do not worry about your life, what you will eat or what you will drink; nor about your body, what you will put on (Matthew 6:25).

Where is God when I want to be filthy rich?
Do not be afraid when one becomes rich, when the glory of his house is increased (Psalm 49:16).

Twenty Ways to Mash Materialism

Here are some great ways to develop a heart that loves God and not stuff:
1. Sponsor a child through Compassion International.

2. Give money to your church.
3. Buy a homeless person lunch.
4. Give away things you don't need.
5. Give away something that would be really hard to give away.
6. Do a Bible study on greed, money, giving, or poverty.
7. List the things that you want and the things that you actually need to live.
8. Buy groceries for a family in need.
9. Have a garage sale and donate the money to a local charity.
10. Take a collection in your youth group for a special cause.
11. Offer to do chores for an older person.
12. Visit people in your neighborhood or church whose ability to leave home is limited.
13. Baby-sit for free the children of a single parent.
14. Ask your parents and friends what they think about materialism.
15. Research the whole topic of materialism, and write a report about it.
16. Start a club on campus designed to help low-income families.
17. Offer to help at a local soup kitchen or thrift store.
18. Make two piles in your room (stuff I need and stuff I want) and see what you learn.
19. Go to a homeless shelter with your youth group. Interview a homeless person and ask what it's like to be homeless.
20. See what it's like to live without your allowance for one month.

Creating Your Own Financial Empire

(Self-Employment)

Self-employment is great if you have a lot of work. Self-employment has all sorts of benefits. You can set your own schedule. You're your own boss. You have a say in how much you get paid and the freedom to create your own financial empire. But being your own boss can also create headaches that can lead you to dishonesty, a loss of integrity, and halfhearted attempts at starting what you promised to finish. The Bible talks about being responsible and keeping your word even if you lose money on a big deal. In God's eyes, it's better to be an honest out-of-work person than a dishonest slime who's reeling in the bucks.

Where is God when I have friends who deal drugs and it seems like an easy way to make a lot of quick money?

Do not let your heart envy sinners, but be zealous for the fear of the LORD all the day (Proverbs 23:17).

Where is God when I make a lot of money detailing cars, but I don't want to pay any income tax?

For because of this you also pay taxes, for they are God's ministers attending continually to this very thing (Romans 13:6).

Where is God when the woman I do yard work for always asks me to do extra chores, but she doesn't pay for the additional tasks?

The LORD repay your work, and a full reward be given you by the LORD God of Israel, under whose wings you have come for refuge (Ruth 2:12).

Where is God when I clean homes on the weekends and I am often tempted to steal?

Lest I be full and deny You, and say, "Who is the LORD?" Or lest I be poor and steal, and profane the name of my God (Proverbs 30:9).

Where is God when the kids I baby-sit are into physical and mental torture? Help!

That this is a rebellious people, lying children, children who will not hear the law of the LORD (Isaiah 30:9).

Where is God when I want to know why He wants me to be honest with my money?

Lying lips are an abomination to the LORD, but those who deal truthfully are His delight (Proverbs 12:22).

Your Attitude Stinks

(Working on Your Attitude)

How bad does your attitude smell? Does it penetrate the olfactory nerves of salivating slugs in a seeping sewer? Can your boss smell it the moment he asks you to spray out a few disgusting trashcans? Bad attitudes at work create hassles. Hassles for your coworkers. Hassles for your boss. And most of all, hassles for you. Any boss sincerely concerned for the business won't tolerate a teenager whose attitude clearly affects job performance.

So what can you do when you know your attitude smells like the bowels of a trash truck? Pray. Take a time-out. Pray. Catch your breath and count to a thousand. Pray. Ask for two weeks' paid vacation. Pray.

Talking to God is your only hope. Well, maybe not your only hope, but certainly the best.

Where is God when I hate work?
And whatever you do in word or deed, do all in the name of the Lord Jesus, giving thanks to God the Father through Him (Colossians 3:17).

Where is God when I can't stand trimming trees?
If a tree falls to the south or the north, in the place where the tree falls, there it shall lie (Ecclesiastes 11:3).

Where is God when I'm always complaining at work? I know I need to change, but what does God say?
Do all things without complaining and disputing (Philippians 2:14).

Where is God when I work in a movie theater and I always have to pick up the trash on the floor?

He takes away the understanding of the chiefs of the people of the earth, and makes them wander in a pathless wilderness (Job 12:24).

Where is God when I struggle with being lazy on the job?
In all labor there is profit, but idle chatter leads only to poverty (Proverbs 14:23).

Where is God when I have to do all the grunt work?
For it is better, if it is the will of God, to suffer for doing good than for doing evil (1 Peter 3:17).

Where is God when my attitude toward work needs some improvement?
This is the covenant that I will make with them after those days, says the LORD: I will put My laws into their hearts, and in their minds I will write them (Hebrews 10:16).

Service with a Smile

(Being a Servant)

If you're going to smile at your customers, please make sure it's the real thing. People appreciate sincerity, but most can tell if your smile is a thinly disguised attempt to pretend you care about them. You can give an honest smile, even if your customers bark like wild dogs, when you learn what it means to be humble. When you're humble, you don't have to be right. You don't have to prove yourself or show a customer that you've got a sharper, quicker tongue than he does. You can take a hit to your ego, deflect it with the patience that comes only from God, and return a smile—not wanting or needing anything in return. And that's the type of humility that makes God smile.

Where is God when I have to explain to a customer why there's a dead fly in her salad?

Behold, I will send swarms of flies on you (Exodus 8:21).

Where is God when I want to know how to make my work meaningful?
Therefore, whether you eat or drink, or whatever you do, do all to the glory of God (1 Corinthians 10:31).

Where is God when the majority of customers are pushy and impatient?
He who is slow to wrath has great understanding, but he who is impulsive exalts folly (Proverbs 14:29).

Where is God when I'm forced to be nice to a customer I can't stand?
With good will doing service, as to the Lord, and not to men (Ephesians 6:7).

Where is God when a customer accuses me of being rude to her? How should I respond?
A soft answer turns away wrath, but a harsh word stirs up anger (Proverbs 15:1).

Where is God when I have a hard time helping people who treat me as if I'm their personal slave? What can I do to be more like Christ?
But as you abound in everything—in faith, in speech, in knowledge, in all diligence, and in your love for us—see that you abound in this grace also (2 Corinthians 8:7).

Where is God when I wonder about Christ's attitude toward serving others?
If I then, your Lord and Teacher, have washed your feet, you also ought to wash one another's feet (John 13:14).

Where is God when my job seems like slavery instead of service?
And I thank Christ Jesus our Lord who has enabled me, because He counted me faithful, putting me into the ministry (1 Timothy 1:12).

Chapter NINE

Cross-Training
Your Faith

BARBED WIRE. *SUCK sand and stay low*. Thirty-foot cargo nets. *Slip and you'll die*. Climbing walls. *Without safety nets*. Rope climbs. Rope ladders. Rope swings. *Rope burns*. Rolling logs. *Don't land in the middle*. Four-story towers with no stairs. *How you get up is your problem*. A 150-foot rope connected from the four-story tower to a 10-foot pole. *You go first. No, really, I insist!* Monkey bars. *A little bit harder than the ones at the playground*. Ten-foot walls. Twelve-foot walls. Fourteen-foot walls. *Bring a ladder.*

Does all this reading make you tired? Welcome to the Navy SEAL team obstacle course on Coronado Island, San Diego. If you're a civilian like the rest of us, completing the course takes about, oh, let's say one to two hours. If you're a SEAL, the first time you do the course, you have less than eleven minutes. Each week you need to beat your time, or you'll be sorry you didn't. Really sorry. The SEAL trainers take their job very seriously. They're out to train one of the most elite forces in the armed services. Forget about what you've seen in the movie theaters. We don't know what they really do. But you can be certain about one thing: A Navy SEAL is the ultimate cross-trainer.

A person who cross-trains is someone who practices different sports to develop strength and stamina in various muscle groups. Cross-training adds creativity to workouts, increases overall conditioning, and eliminates boring repetition found in training for only one sport. Cross-training works. It strengthens weaknesses to improve the overall performance of the athlete.

172

For a Christian and an athlete, cross-training is essential. A football player doesn't just lift weights. A Christian doesn't just pray. A baseball player does more than catch fly balls. A Christian does more than talk about faith. A water polo player swims more than laps. A Christian gives more than money. Cross-training strengthens an athlete's physical condition. Getting in spiritual shape strengthens and prepares a Christian to be who God designed the individual to be.

Teenagers who cross-train their faith by participating in God's training program have an incredible opportunity to use their athletic abilities to share their faith. Athletics is an international language everybody understands. Sad, but true, sports have a bigger following than God. Students who practice their faith on the field can let their friends know where their abilities and strength come from. I've seen high-school athletes with Philippians 4:13 on their jerseys, letterman's jackets, cheerleading uniforms, or shoes: "I can do all things through Christ who strengthens me." Not even a muscle-building protein drink offers that type of strength.

An Athlete's Foot Attitude

(Attitude Adjustments)

It smells. It reeks. That odor is your attitude and we've all had one like yours before. Throwing tennis rackets, golf clubs, and helmets. Shot-putting bowling balls after hurling three gutter balls in a row. A bad attitude can ruin your game. It can also ruin your partner's game and cause you to lose the whole match. Then you won't be the only one with a bad attitude. Bad attitudes spread like an oil spill, staining and ruining everything in their path.

OK, so you're having a bad day. Everyone does once in a while, but before your attitude heads downwind, think of how it makes others feel. You're stressed out. Are you going to make everyone else upset, too? Take a time-out. Get a drink of water. There's nothing you can do about the ball you just hit out. But you can change your attitude. Try it. It'll make a big difference and you'll enjoy your game a lot more. I know winning's important, but you gotta start with a winning attitude 'cause they don't sell deodorant for bad ones.

Where is God when I know He has given me a lot of athletic ability, but I'm not sure how to handle all the praise I get?
When pride comes, then comes shame; but with the humble is wisdom (Proverbs 11:2).

Where is God when my coach tells me that I'd be more coachable if I would change my negative attitude?
By pride comes nothing but strife, but with the well-advised is wisdom (Proverbs 13:10).

Where is God when I'm tempted to want to rub a victory in an opponent's face?
Pride goes before destruction, and a haughty spirit before a fall (Proverbs 16:18).

Where is God when a guy on my team thinks he's so great, but he drives everyone else crazy?
For if anyone thinks himself to be something, when he is nothing, he deceives himself (Galatians 6:3).

Where is God when I want to have a positive impact on my teammates, but I can't stand the coach?
Do all things without complaining and disputing (Philippians 2:14).

Where is God when I struggle with having a godly attitude while I'm on the court? How can God's Word change my attitude?
For the word of God is living and powerful, and sharper than any two-edged sword, piercing even to the division of soul and spirit, and of joints and marrow, and is a discerner of the thoughts and intents of the heart (Hebrews 4:12).

Where is God when my teammates are totally selfish?

For where envy and self-seeking exist, confusion and every evil thing are there (James 3:16).

Where is God when I can't understand why the best player on my team is the biggest jerk?
A man who isolates himself seeks his own desire; he rages against all wise judgment (Proverbs 18:1).

Be a Team Player

(Teamwork)

Being a team player is a very important part of living out your faith on the court, track, field, or gym floor. People will see Christ in you if you look to their interests and the team's best interests. No one wants to be a loser, but people who can't be team players are already on the losing team. Being a team player doesn't mean you have to be a rah-rah cheerleader or mascot. You just need to be willing to give your best, be humble, and do whatever it takes to make the team look good (without cheating, of course!). People on the court and off the court are looking for a reason to live. Athletics is just one of the many areas young people put in their lives before God. You can help put God in their lives by putting Him first, them second, and yourself third. When you put yourself in third place, you're the type of team player God wants on His team.

Where is God when I get jealous of my teammates who play better than I do?
But let each one examine his own work, and then he will have rejoicing in himself alone, and not in another (Galatians 6:4).

Where is God when all my teammates are Christians, but we can't work together?
Submitting to one another in the fear of God (Ephesians 5:21).

Where is God when I want to be a better encourager to my teammates?

As iron sharpens iron, so a man sharpens the countenance of his friend (Proverbs 27:17).

Where is God when there's a lot of squabbling on my team?
Let us not become conceited, provoking one another, envying one another (Galatians 5:26).

Where is God when everyone on my team is really discouraged because we're doing so badly?
That their hearts may be encouraged, being knit together in love, and attaining to all riches of the full assurance of understanding, to the knowledge of the mystery of God, both of the Father and of Christ (Colossians 2:2).

Where is God when my team is great on the court but lousy off the court?
Finally, all of you be of one mind, having compassion for one another; love as brothers, be tenderhearted, be courteous (1 Peter 3:8).

Where is God when I don't want to get caught up in all the "attitudes" on my team?
All of you be submissive to one another, and be clothed with humility, for "God resists the proud, but gives grace to the humble" (1 Peter 5:5).

Where is God when I have trouble loving one of my teammates who's really conceited?
Beloved, if God so loved us, we also ought to love one another (1 John 4:11).

Don't Give Up

(Perseverance)

You don't need to be a great athlete to go out for cross-country. You need two legs, a set of lungs, a knack for pain, and a stretcher at the finish line. I coached cross-country for three years at Dana

Hills High School in Dana Point, California. I really didn't know much about the sport. The head coach gave me a group of sophomore guys and a lesson in life: To cross the finish line, you've got to be moving.

The same is true for following Jesus Christ. The Christian life is a race. The path is straight and narrow, the goal is Jesus Christ, and the prize is eternal life. It's a race filled with adventures, hills and valleys, pressures, and sideaches. Whatever you do, don't give up. It's the only race in this life worth running. When you get in the habit of giving up, quitting becomes easier and easier. Pretty soon you become numb to what it means to keep a commitment. You may have all sorts of reasons for quitting, but the only one who loses is you. God can give you all the energy, strength, power, courage, endurance, and oxygen you need to hang in there, but even He won't keep you from quitting. He's spread the tape across the finish, and He's cheering you along the whole way. When you feel like giving up, give yourself up to God and trust Him to get you to the finish.

Where is God when I feel like quitting, but I know I need to press on?
I have fought the good fight, I have finished the race, I have kept the faith (2 Timothy 4:7).

Where is God when I can't understand why God allowed me to get injured right before a big game?
And not only that, but we also glory in tribulations, knowing that tribulation produces perseverance; and perseverance, character; and character, hope (Romans 5:3–4).

Where is God when I need His strength to keep me from losing my cool?
Now may the Lord direct your hearts into the love of God and into the patience of Christ (2 Thessalonians 3:5).

Where is God when I get easily discouraged because I'm not a very good athlete?

Therefore we also, since we are surrounded by so great a cloud of witnesses, let us lay aside every weight, and the sin which so easily ensnares us, and let us run with endurance the race that is set before us (Hebrews 12:1).

Where is God when my coach knows I'm a Christian and he says things just to get a reaction out of me?

My brethren, count it all joy when you fall into various trials, knowing that the testing of your faith produces patience. But let patience have its perfect work, that you may be perfect and complete, lacking nothing (James 1:2–4).

Where is God when I want to know how I can be a good witness to my teammates?

But also for this very reason, giving all diligence, add to your faith virtue, to virtue knowledge, to knowledge self-control, to self-control perseverance, to perseverance godliness, to godliness brotherly kindness, and to brotherly kindness love (2 Peter 1:5–7).

Where is God when my coach doesn't see how hard I'm trying?

Remembering without ceasing your work of faith, labor of love, and patience of hope in our Lord Jesus Christ in the sight of our God and Father (1 Thessalonians 1:3).

Where is God when it's really hard living like a Christian around my teammates?

But none of these things move me; nor do I count my life dear to myself, so that I may finish my race with joy, and the ministry which I received from the Lord Jesus, to testify to the gospel of the grace of God (Acts 20:24).

Feeling Like a Failure

(Failing)

Everybody loses. I don't care what anyone says. Everyone, at one time or another, loses at something. It could be a game, competition, relationship, class, or driving test. Everyone fails. However, there's a big difference between failing and losing. You could lose the best match of your life and know you played your very best. That's not failure. Or you could win an easy competition and feel like a complete loser.

God understands how you feel when you lose. He also knows what's going on inside you when you feel like a failure. He knows how your self-esteem can be too closely tied to your win-loss record. That's why He wants you to find your security in Him, not in your trophies or medals. He's more interested in how you feel about yourself and your friendship with Him than any school records you hope to set. The pressure to succeed can squish your self-esteem and leave you pinned under the weight of insecurity. God's Word says that we are more than conquerors through Him who loved us. In Jesus Christ, you are not a failure or a loser. You're a winner.

Where is God when I blew the winning shot and none of my teammates will talk to me?

Keep my soul, and deliver me; let me not be ashamed, for I put my trust in You (Psalm 25:20).

Where is God when I struggle with making winning more important than it is?

For what profit is it to a man if he gains the whole world, and is himself destroyed or lost? (Luke 9:25).

Where is God when I get really depressed by a loss?

Therefore we do not lose heart. Even though our outward man is perishing, yet the inward man is being renewed day by day (2 Corinthians 4:16).

Where is God when I wonder if Jesus ever felt like a loser?

For consider Him who endured such hostility from sinners against Himself, lest you become weary and discouraged in your souls (Hebrews 12:3).

Where is God when I feel like a complete failure anytime I lose? Does God love me even when I fail?

My mercy I will keep for him forever, and My covenant shall stand firm with him (Psalm 89:28).

Where is God when I'm in a slump and I need God's help to pull me out?

But the LORD is with me as a mighty, awesome One (Jeremiah 20:11).

Where is God when I don't want winning to become more important than my relationship with God?

He who loves his life will lose it, and he who hates his life in this world will keep it for eternal life (John 12:25).

Where is God when I want to have a good attitude following a loss?

For the Lord GOD will help Me; therefore I will not be disgraced; therefore I have set My face like a flint, and I know that I will not be ashamed (Isaiah 50:7).

Where is God when my dad refuses to talk to me after I lose? Does God accept me even when I lose?

For the Scripture says, "Whoever believes on Him will not be put to shame" (Romans 10:11).

Giving All You've Got

(Best Effort)

One hundred percent. That's what coaches want. One hundred percent is what they expect. They figure if you want to be on the team, you want to win. If you want to win, you've got to train hard. Harder than the next person. Harder than the team who wants to beat you. Coaches want you to give all you've got until you don't got anything left to give. That's why each coach has a set of rules and expectations to make the team as effective as possible. Coaches don't want their time to be wasted, and they're out there to make you a better athlete. Sure, not all coaches are perfect, but they want you to give 100 percent so you can perfect your skills and talents.

Giving all you've got is also a great way to say, "Thanks," to God for the abilities He's given you. When Jesus lived on this earth, He gave all He had to be an example of how to live life on purpose. When you give God all you've got, you're living life on purpose— 100 percent.

Where is God when I'm trying to do my best to be a positive influence on my team, but I get tired of doing it all by myself?
Depart from evil and do good; seek peace and pursue it (Psalm 34:14).

Where is God when I don't feel like trying my hardest because it's easier to cheat?
And also if anyone competes in athletics, he is not crowned unless he competes according to the rules (2 Timothy 2:5).

Where is God when I want to know how I can give Him 100 percent effort in all I do on my team?
But you, O man of God, flee these things and pursue righteousness, godliness, faith, love, patience, gentleness (1 Timothy 6:11).

Where is God when I want to keep from bragging anytime I win?
But God forbid that I should boast except in the cross of our Lord Jesus Christ, by whom the world has been crucified to me, and I to the world (Galatians 6:14).

Where is God when I hear a lot of foul language on my team? How does God want me to act?
Neither filthiness, nor foolish talking, nor coarse jesting, which are not fitting, but rather giving of thanks (Ephesians 5:4).

Where is God when I'm having trouble encouraging others because I'm playing so badly?
Therefore comfort each other and edify one another, just as you also are doing (1 Thessalonians 5:11).

Where is God when I get tired of putting in my best effort? No one else seems to try.

But as for you, brethren, do not grow weary in doing good (2 Thessalonians 3:13).

Where is God when I feel like I'm not giving much effort at practice or in any area of my life?

Be diligent to present yourself approved to God, a worker who does not need to be ashamed, rightly dividing the word of truth (2 Timothy 2:15).

No Looking Back

(Getting Focused)

Missed shot. Dropped ball. Serve out. Field goal wide. Incomplete pass. Out of bounds. Blocked ball. Terrible set. So what are you going to do now? You just blew it. Everybody was watching. You're embarrassed. *That was such an easy shot! How could I have missed that? I'm so lame.*

Dwelling on a bad shot gets you nowhere. I know you've heard it before, but it's true. Look forward, not backward. There's nothing you can do to fix that last shot, but you can always take another one. The only value in looking back is to see what you did wrong, think about it, learn from it, and then drop-kick it out of your mind.

Looking at your mistakes can get you focused on yourself instead of God's forgiveness. When you break God's heart by doing something wrong, admit your sin, ask Him to forgive you, accept His forgiveness, and turn from committing the same mistake again. God doesn't look back, and He doesn't want you to look back, either.

Where is God when I need to forget about my poor performance in my last meet?

Do not remember the former things, nor consider the things of old (Isaiah 43:18).

Where is God when my bad attitude caused us to lose last night? Will God forgive me?
I, even I, am He who blots out your transgressions for My own sake; and I will not remember your sins (Isaiah 43:25).

Where is God when I used to pray before games, but now I don't include Him in anything? Does God still care about me?
The LORD has appeared of old to me, saying, "Yes, I have loved you with an everlasting love; therefore with lovingkindness I have drawn you" (Jeremiah 31:3).

Where is God when I started a fight that got our team disqualified?
Iniquities prevail against me; as for our transgressions, You will provide atonement for them (Psalm 65:3).

Where is God when I recently made a commitment to Christ, but I have a hard time living like a Christian on the court?
But God, who is rich in mercy, because of His great love with which He loved us, even when we were dead in trespasses, made us alive together with Christ (by grace you have been saved) (Ephesians 2:4–5).

Where is God when I need to put my failures behind me and look forward to what He wants to do in my life?
For behold, I create new heavens and a new earth; and the former shall not be remembered or come to mind (Isaiah 65:17).

Where is God when I get so depressed by losing?
Therefore we do not lose heart. Even though our outward man is perishing, yet the inward man is being renewed day by day (2 Corinthians 4:16).

Where is God when I got angry and made a fool of myself at my game last night?

Do not remember the sins of my youth, nor my transgressions; according to Your mercy remember me, for Your goodness' sake, O Lord (Psalm 25:7).

Stiff Competition

(God's Strength)

I'll never forget the time I tried out to be a beach lifeguard in South Orange County. I was up against some muscle-bound guys who looked like they'd been swimming since infancy. I was a senior in high school, and I spent a whole semester in the pool preparing for the tryouts. Two weeks before the tryouts, I got the flu and was in bed for a week and a half. The day of the tryouts came, I hadn't swum in two weeks, and I was in for a dunking. There were only sixty guys trying out for ten spots. *Only sixty!* Even though I was sick, out of shape, and out of hope, I wanted to compete. The race was a half-mile run, half-mile swim, half-mile run. I did well. I finished. Last. Dead last. Dead and last.

Stiff competition is a part of life. There's always going to be someone or some team that is better, stronger, faster, or able to throw locomotives in a single toss. When you're faced with stiff competition and have the gut-level feeling that you know you're going to lose, you've got the advantage. Few people perform best against an easy opponent. The majority of people excel against someone who challenges all their abilities.

Stiff competition is nothing to be afraid of because the Bible promises that you've got the God of the universe on your team. That doesn't mean He's going to flip the scoreboard in your favor when no one's looking. But you have His presence and His strength to help you do your best.

Where is God when our team is going to get killed . . . HELP ME!

Do not fear or be dismayed; tomorrow go out against them, for the LORD is with you (2 Chronicles 20:17).

Where is God when I have trouble being committed to God in the same way I'm committed to my sports?
But reject profane and old wives' fables, and exercise yourself toward godliness (1 Timothy 4:7).

Where is God when it's easy for me to train for my sport, but I'm less committed to spending time alone with God?
And everyone who competes for the prize is temperate in all things. Now they do it to obtain a perishable crown, but we for an imperishable crown (1 Corinthians 9:25).

Where is God when I'm often tempted to cheat in order to win because I'm so competitive?
And also if anyone competes in athletics, he is not crowned unless he competes according to the rules (2 Timothy 2:5).

Where is God when I make the finals of a tournament and ask Him to give me a victory, but He sometimes does and other times doesn't?
The horse is prepared for the day of battle, but deliverance is of the LORD (Proverbs 21:31).

Where is God when I always get sick to my stomach before a big match?
Then all this assembly shall know that the LORD does not save with sword and spear; for the battle is the LORD's, and He will give you into our hands (1 Samuel 17:47).

Where is God when I need His help to face an opponent I've lost to before?
For I, the LORD your God, will hold your right hand, saying to you, "Fear not, I will help you" (Isaiah 41:13).

Where is God when I don't get to play much in games and I wonder if it's really worth it?

Therefore I run thus: not with uncertainty. Thus I fight: not as one who beats the air (1 Corinthians 9:26).

The Pain of Discipline

(Developing Discipline)

Clicking the channel changer is so easy, so painless, so natural. It doesn't cause blisters, sore arms, bruised shins, or aching backs. The remote control is a technological wonder of modern society.

Flipping the channel may work for watching your favorite programs. But living by remote control, avoiding the pain and purpose of discipline, creates more chaos than comfort. Too many athletes do things just because a coach tells them to, but they never develop personal discipline. That's remote control living. *Discipline* comes from the word *disciple*, which means "learner." People who discipline themselves in any area of life are "learning" how to live.

Discipline happens in various ways. Hitting the snooze button once instead of three times. Getting to practice on time. Taking the nets down before your coach tells you to. Holding your tongue when you feel like ranting and raving. Keeping promises. Saying no when you feel like saying yes. Eating right. Reading the Bible. Doing ten more push-ups. Accepting pain before pleasure.

A good friend asked me, "Do you want to live with the pain of discipline or the agony of regret?" That's a good way to look at life. How many of us live life saying to ourselves, "I should've, could've, would've . . ."? The pain of discipline keeps us learning what God has in store for us. We become lifelong learners instead of lifelong losers. Yes, discipline is painful, but it yields great rewards. Turn on discipline and turn off the tube. Click!

Where is God when I can't stand difficult practices?

Now no chastening seems to be joyful for the present, but painful;

nevertheless, afterward it yields the peaceable fruit of righteousness to those who have been trained by it (Hebrews 12:11).

Where is God when I want to be a great tennis player, but I don't want to work for it?

The soul of a lazy man desires, and has nothing; but the soul of the diligent shall be made rich (Proverbs 13:4).

Where is God when I want to be as strong a Christian as I am an athlete?

Exercise yourself toward godliness (1 Timothy 4:7).

Where is God when my teammates never take practice seriously?

The fear of the LORD is the beginning of knowledge, but fools despise wisdom and instruction (Proverbs 1:7).

Where is God when my coach is always after me to work harder?

And you mourn at last, when your flesh and your body are consumed, and say: "How I have hated instruction, and my heart despised correction! I have not obeyed the voice of my teachers, nor inclined my ear to those who instructed me!" (Proverbs 5:11–13).

Where is God when guys on my team goof off anytime I do? How can I help the team instead of hurt it?

He who keeps instruction is in the way of life, but he who refuses correction goes astray (Proverbs 10:17).

Where is God when I get really angry with my coach for telling me what to do?

Whoever loves instruction loves knowledge, but he who hates correction is stupid (Proverbs 12:1).

Where is God when I can't understand why we have hard workouts if we're still going to lose?

If you endure chastening, God deals with you as with sons; for what son is there whom a father does not chasten? (Hebrews 12:7).

Where is God when my coach tells me I talk too much in practice?

In all labor there is profit, but idle chatter leads only to poverty (Proverbs 14:23).

Totally Focused

(Concentration)

A personal commitment to Jesus Christ gives an athlete an edge over the competition. God created you with physical, mental, social, and spiritual capacities to know Him and involve Him in every area of your life. He created you for Himself, not the other way around. Knowing Jesus Christ won't necessarily make you a better athlete, but it will give you access to the One with all power, all strength, all endurance, all creativity, and everything else He is. Jesus Christ can help you focus your concentration on Him instead of yourself. In the struggle and pressure of competition, you can pray to the God who hears all your prayers and who cares about you. When no one shows up at your games, God is there, and He's your number one cheerleader.

Where is God when I want to realize where my abilities and talents come from?
Not that we are sufficient of ourselves to think of anything as being from ourselves, but our sufficiency is from God (2 Corinthians 3:5).

Where is God when I want to have a Christlike attitude on the court?
Make me walk in the path of Your commandments, for I delight in it (Psalm 119:35).

Where is God when in the heat of competition, I sometimes do things I know are wrong?
Direct my steps by Your word, and let no iniquity have dominion over me (Psalm 119:133).

Where is God when I need to have an attitude check before I walk on the court?
Examine yourselves as to whether you are in the faith. Test yourselves (2 Corinthians 13:5).

Where is God when I need His Word to help focus me when I compete?
Therefore you shall lay up these words of mine in your heart and in your soul, and bind them as a sign on your hand, and they shall be as frontlets between your eyes (Deuteronomy 11:18).

Where is God when I have a foul mouth on the court and I need help changing it?
Put away from you a deceitful mouth, and put perverse lips far from you (Proverbs 4:24).

Where is God when I get really anxious before a match and I have trouble focusing?
Keep your heart with all diligence, for out of it spring the issues of life (Proverbs 4:23).

Where is God when my thoughts can get really negative as I lose points? How can I be more positive?
Therefore, holy brethren, partakers of the heavenly calling, consider the Apostle and High Priest of our confession, Christ Jesus (Hebrews 3:1).

Where is God when I have trouble concentrating during my races because I get so distracted?
Looking unto Jesus, the author and finisher of our faith, who for the joy that was set before Him endured the cross, despising the shame, and has sat down at the right hand of the throne of God (Hebrews 12:2).

Getting Your Mouth in Shape

For some athletes, the tongue can be the most difficult muscle to get in shape. In a fit of rage, when you've just made a terrible shot or someone didn't carry out a play the way it was supposed to be done, that little wet hunk of muscle can easily slip a few foul words right past your teeth.

Why do we let our tongues say things that can lead to embarrassment, hurt feelings, harsh looks, team disintegration, and being thrown out of the game? The tongue is an indicator, a sort of scoreboard of what's going on inside the heart and mind. When Jesus spoke about the tongue, He also was speaking about the heart: "Out of the abundance of the heart the mouth speaks" (Matthew 12:34).

Spouting off can get you benched or kicked out of the game. It can cause you to lose your concentration even more than you already have. What are some ways to keep your tongue in your mouth and your mind on your game?

- **Do pregame prep**. Think about your attitude, game, and actions before you get on the court. Ask God to help you watch what you say.
- **Have a game partner**. Ask a friend, particularly a Christian friend, to pray for you as you play. Ask the person to help you keep your tongue in shape. Before you compete, pray together about setting an example for Christ.
- **Focus on Scripture**. Memorize a short, favorite Scripture to think about during the breaks between plays. Suggested verses include Philippians 3:14; Psalm 118:14; Hebrews 12:2; 2 Timothy 4:7; 1 Corinthians 9:24; and Philippians 4:13.
- **Apologize**. OK, so everything you just did to avoid shooting off your mouth didn't work. Own up to it; say you're sorry to God and to anyone you may have hurt or offended. Saying you're sorry isn't a sign of weakness; it's a Christlike example of honesty and integrity.
- **Be patient**. Change doesn't happen overnight. Just like it takes months to get in excellent shape, it takes a long time to change bad habits. Spend some time in James 3, and ask God to give you the desire and strength to be His person on and off the court.

Unsportsmanlike Conduct

(Temper Tantrums)

"You're outta here!" I never got thrown out of a game, but I've seen plenty of guys who have been. It's not a pretty sight. Chairs fly through the air as the disgruntled athlete grunts and huffs his way to the locker room. Clipboards slam on the ground. Penalty points are awarded to the other team. A certain victory becomes questionable. Unsportsmanlike conduct may be great show for the audience, but it doesn't do the team much good. Or your relationship with God. People are watching to see if your life as a Christian really means something. On the court, some Christians make more dents in God's kingdom than actual differences. So what do you do when you feel like you want to rip the ears off your opponent or the referee? How do you stay in control while competing?

Keeping your cool happens before you even get on the court. It's called getting mentally prepared. It's also the time to get spiritually prepared. You're not only going to battle your physical opponent. You're also up against your spiritual opponent, the devil. The Bible promises that "He who is in you is greater than he who is in the world" (1 John 4:4). God will protect you from Satan getting the edge on your emotions. The Bible says not to give Satan a foothold. That means don't give him anything to boost him up because he'll try to trip you up.

Spend some time praying about your match, and ask God to give you His grace to practice His presence on the court. Ask Him to protect you from saying something you might regret. Tell Him you need His strength to help you focus on Him. Ask Him to help you forget about bad calls so you can concentrate on the next point. Ask Him to help you do what you need to do for His glory.

Where is God when I battle trying to control my temper toward the referee?

For the flesh lusts against the Spirit, and the Spirit against the flesh; and these are contrary to one another, so that you do not do the things that you wish (Galatians 5:17).

Where is God when I scream at my teammates because I hate losing?
Hatred stirs up strife, but love covers all sins (Proverbs 10:12).

Where is God when I have trouble controlling my anger on the court?
A wrathful man stirs up strife, but he who is slow to anger allays contention (Proverbs 15:18).

Where is God when my Christian team is plagued with bad attitudes?
Now may the God of patience and comfort grant you to be like-minded toward one another, according to Christ Jesus (Romans 15:5).

Where is God when I need help getting along with my teammates?
Bearing with one another, and forgiving one another, if anyone has a complaint against another; even as Christ forgave you, so you also must do. But above all these things put on love, which is the bond of perfection (Colossians 3:13–14).

Where is God when my coach and I disagree on practically everything?
The beginning of strife is like releasing water; therefore stop contention before a quarrel starts (Proverbs 17:14).

Where is God when my teammates and I argue constantly?
But avoid foolish and ignorant disputes, knowing that they generate strife (2 Timothy 2:23).

Win at All Costs?

(Ego Trips)

Cutthroat competition brings out the worst in us. Well, most of us. If you're a highly competitive person and winning is tops on your priority list, you probably live for challenge. Or you are willing to die for a good challenge. Our society holds up winners and shuns losers. Losing isn't very socially acceptable in this day and age. But the win-at-all-costs attitude sometimes produces more heartache than it's worth.

A guy who is hypercompetitive usually learns it from his dad, who's so insecure that he needs to compete with his son to prove himself. A dad who throws tennis rackets produces a teen who throws 'em farther. These people aren't a whole lot of fun. For the person who has to win at all costs, whether through throwing tantrums, cheating, or acting like a rabid beast, the hard outside is probably hiding an insecure and scared inside. Poor self-esteem is pretty stiff competition. To beat poor self-esteem, the person has to first hide it and then try to prove how good she really is by winning all the time at any cost. At that price, winning isn't worth it.

The only guy I've ever known with a good win-at-all-costs attitude is Jesus Christ. The only thing really worth winning is eternal life, but we can't win that on our own. That's why I like Jesus' style. He won eternal life without chucking helmets or screaming at the ref. He won eternal life by conquering sin and death through His death and resurrection. He wanted to win for you. He won to overcome lousy self-esteems. He won to defeat the steaming pressure you put on yourself to win. He won so you could win eternal life for free. Eternal life is the one thing you don't have to earn. Jesus Christ already won it. It's a victory that costs you nothing. It's a free gift that makes you free.

Where is God when I need help making my relationship with Him and others more important than winning?

Let not mercy and truth forsake you; bind them around your neck, write them on the tablet of your heart, and so find favor and high esteem in the sight of God and man (Proverbs 3:3–4).

Where is God when my parents put tremendous pressure on me to win? I end up trying to please them instead of God.
For do I now persuade men, or God? Or do I seek to please men? For if I still pleased men, I would not be a bondservant of Christ (Galatians 1:10).

Where is God when I need help remembering who allows me to win my matches?
For the LORD your God is He who goes with you, to fight for you against your enemies, to save you (Deuteronomy 20:4).

Where is God when I try to bring attention to myself when I win? How can I remember to give glory to God?
Therefore, whether you eat or drink, or whatever you do, do all to the glory of God (1 Corinthians 10:31).

Where is God when my friends tell me that I'm too competitive?
With all lowliness and gentleness, with longsuffering, bearing with one another in love (Ephesians 4:2).

Where is God when I'm so set on winning that I shoot my mouth off?
Whoever guards his mouth and tongue keeps his soul from troubles (Proverbs 21:23).

Where is God when I wonder if I can be a winner for Him even when I lose?
But thanks be to God, who gives us the victory through our Lord Jesus Christ (1 Corinthians 15:57).

Where is God when I want to make my faith more important than winning?
For whatever is born of God overcomes the world. And this is the victory that has overcome the world—our faith (1 John 5:4).

Chapter TEN

Future Fears

ONE OF MY favorite places to go running is Doheny Beach Road. It's a beautiful stretch of beach filled with volleyball courts, campgrounds, and barbecue pits. One evening while I was jogging at Doheny, I noticed a group of more than seventy people around a bonfire. Some were standing, talking in groups of three or four. A few people were cooking hamburgers and serving dinner. Others were sitting down, listening to someone who had stood up to talk. And more people were driving in to join the group. People were greeting each other with big bear hugs.

It didn't look like your average beach party. By the way everyone was dressed, it was obvious they came from different economic backgrounds. Teenagers, middle-agers, and older-agers, the gathering was a definite mixed salad. Everyone appeared to be having a great time, but I noticed right away that no one was drinking.

I was intrigued. I'd never seen such a group before at the beach. A spirit of life and enthusiasm permeated the air. It was as if each one had been set free from some dark, horrible experience. They were all different, yet somehow, all the same. Some shared experience had bonded them. They were now a laughing community of friends throwing a party in honor of life.

For a few minutes, I couldn't figure out what the group was all about, but then something in my head clicked: AA. It was an Alcoholics Anonymous meeting. Their differences, smiles, and laughter all made sense to me. The people had a reason to celebrate. For some, it was probably their first party without drugs or alcohol.

They were celebrating their sobriety, a chance to live drug-free and alcohol-free lives. They were ready to live again.

One day at a time. That's the way people in AA try to look at life. You can't do anything to change the past. Who knows what the future holds? The road to recovery happens one day at a time. Wouldn't it be wonderful if we all looked at life like that? The past is gone. We can't predict the future. All we have is today. Jesus said to His followers,

> Therefore do not worry, saying, "What shall we eat?" or "What shall we drink?" or "What shall we wear?" For after all these things the Gentiles seek. For your heavenly Father knows that you need all these things. But seek first the kingdom of God and His righteousness, and all these things shall be added to you. Therefore do not worry about tomorrow, for tomorrow will worry about its own things. Sufficient for the day is its own trouble (Matthew 6:31–34).

Live one day at a time. Do what Jesus says. Rest in God's promises and in His peace today. He's not asking you to ignore your problems or pretend they don't exist. He just wants you to lay them at the foot of Jesus' cross so you can experience the freedom and power of His resurrection. You can celebrate life in Jesus Christ only today.

Blind Faith

(Living by Faith)

Faith and blindness are two different things, but many people want to lump 'em together like camels and humps, dogs and tails, bananas and peels. Blindness is the inability to see. Darkness. Pitch black. The Bible says that faith is believing in the things we can't see.

Every day, you believe in things you can't see—important stuff like air, sound, microwaves, and radio waves. Next time you're eating a TV dinner (microwave and heat rays) while watching your favorite TV show via satellite with the volume blaring (radio waves) as you inhale and exhale (oxygen), ask yourself, Am I living by faith? Am I blind to believe in something that's helping me to exist at this very moment? Can you live without faith that air exists? No way. Can you live without believing in the Creator of air and the very One who created your lungs to be filled with something you can't see? Hmmm . . . *is that blind faith?*

Where is God when I don't have a clue about what faith really is?
Now faith is the substance of things hoped for, the evidence of things not seen (Hebrews 11:1).

Where is God when I want to know how I can please Him with my faith?
But without faith it is impossible to please Him, for he who comes to God must believe that He is, and that He is a rewarder of those who diligently seek Him (Hebrews 11:6).

Where is God when I want to trust Him more and not listen to my doubts?
So Jesus answered and said to them, "Assuredly, I say to you, if you have faith and do not doubt, you will not only do what was done to the fig tree, but also if you say to this mountain, 'Be removed and be cast into the sea,' it will be done" (Matthew 21:21).

Where is God when I'm confused about who to put my faith in?
So Jesus answered and said to them, "Have faith in God" (Mark 11:22).

Where is God when it seems I never have enough faith in Him? Will He give me more faith if I ask?
And the apostles said to the Lord, "Increase our faith." So the Lord said, "If you have faith as a mustard seed, you can say to this mulberry tree, 'Be pulled up by the roots and be planted in the sea,' and it would obey you" (Luke 17:5–6).

Where is God when I want to do great things for Him, but I'm afraid my life won't amount to anything?
Most assuredly, I say to you, he who believes in Me, the works that I do he will do also; and greater works than these he will do, because I go to My Father (John 14:12).

Where is God when I don't know much about the Bible, but I want my faith to grow?
So then faith comes by hearing, and hearing by the word of God (Romans 10:17).

Where is God when it's hard for me to understand what it means to trust Him if I can't see Him?
For we walk by faith, not by sight (2 Corinthians 5:7).

Can God Keep a Promise?

(Trusting God)

I promise I won't tell anyone. I promise to meet you at eight o'clock sharp. I promise I'll never date anybody but you. I promise I'll be your best friend forever. Yeah, right! You hear promises made and promises broken all the time. Why can't people just tell the truth and really mean what they say? *I'll try not to tell anyone, but if what you tell me is really juicy, then I'll probably tell a couple of friends. I'll be late. You are one of many girls I'd love to date. I'm sick of hanging out with you.* A lot of pain and grief could be avoided if people would say what they mean and mean what they say. But life doesn't work like that. You've heard it before. Good intentions. People really mean well, but they can't seem to get their act together. They'd keep a promise and stick to their commitments if they knew what a real commitment is. Right? Wrong. You're tired of broken promises.

God is sick of broken promises, too. He hears them all the time. But you know what? Despite all the broken promises He hears (including a bunch of our own), He continues to love and be faithful to those who can't seem to keep their word. God's Word is filled with literally thousands of promises (that's what this book is all about!) so you can experience a radical friendship with your heavenly Father. If you've been let down by others and you feel like you can't trust anyone, go to God and see if He'll keep His promises. You'll be amazed at what you discover.

Where is God when I can't seem to trust anybody? Why should I trust God?

God is not a man, that He should lie, nor a son of man, that He should repent (Numbers 23:19).

Where is God when I want to know if anyone else has wondered whether God keeps His promises?

Now, O LORD God, the word which You have spoken concerning Your servant and concerning his house, establish it forever and do as You have said (2 Samuel 7:25).

Where is God when I think about the many times I let Him down, but He never lets me down?

You have performed Your words, for You are righteous (Nehemiah 9:8).

Where is God when I want to develop a greater love for God's promises?

I rejoice at Your word as one who finds great treasure (Psalm 119:162).

Where is God when my faith is so weak? Will God promise to strengthen my faith if I ask Him?

He did not waver at the promise of God through unbelief, but was strengthened in faith, giving glory to God, and being fully convinced that what He had promised He was also able to perform (Romans 4:20–21).

Where is God when I can't understand why He is so slow in answering my prayers?

The Lord is not slack concerning His promise, as some count slackness, but is longsuffering toward us, not willing that any should perish but that all should come to repentance (2 Peter 3:9).

Where is God when I'm always breaking my promises to Him?
Turn away my eyes from looking at worthless things, and revive me in Your way. Establish Your word to Your servant, who is devoted to fearing You (Psalm 119:37–38).

Where is God when I'm amazed at all of His promises I find in the Bible?
By which have been given to us exceedingly great and precious promises, that through these you may be partakers of the divine nature (2 Peter 1:4).

Confidence Killers

(Regaining Your Confidence)

Whoops! You blew it again. Can you believe you muffed the final shot? You studied all night long and you got a *D*. Why would your boyfriend be such a jerk to you in front of all your friends? You got a great award in a music contest, but your mom said a few notes needed work. *What is wrong with this world? Why is everyone out to get me?* Confidence killers. They stalk you. Nasty voices running inside your head tell you you're no good, you'll never measure up.

Confidence killers can destroy how you feel about yourself and how you feel about others. Confidence killers can also demolish your relationship with God. You have an enemy named Satan who's got a detailed game plan to destroy your confidence in God.

If you're feeling timid, weak, and insecure, and your confidence is about as high as the curb, remember that God believes in you even when you don't believe in yourself. Having God's strength can give you a tremendous amount of courage to tackle any negative thought, feeling, or insecurity. He believes in you like no one else does!

Where is God when I seem to lack confidence in just about every area of my life?

For You are my hope, O Lord GOD; You are my trust from my youth (Psalm 71:5).

Where is God when I'm afraid that sudden tragedy is going to strike me, my friends, or my family?

Do not be afraid of sudden terror, nor of trouble from the wicked when it comes; for the LORD will be your confidence, and will keep your foot from being caught (Proverbs 3:25–26).

Where is God when the very thought of approaching Him intimidates me?

In whom we have boldness and access with confidence through faith in Him (Ephesians 3:12).

Where is God when I feel like I'm not as confident in my relationship with Him as I used to be?

For we have become partakers of Christ if we hold the beginning of our confidence steadfast to the end (Hebrews 3:14).

Where is God when I want to know why I should place my confidence in Him?

Let us therefore come boldly to the throne of grace, that we may obtain mercy and find grace to help in time of need (Hebrews 4:16).

Where is God when I'm afraid to talk to Him? Will He even listen to me?

Now this is the confidence that we have in Him, that if we ask anything according to His will, He hears us (1 John 5:14).

For Upperclassmen Only

Just last June, you and the rest of the senior class were frothing at the mouth like chained bloodhounds waiting for graduation. Now that fall is here, life looks a lot different. Some students go to a four-year college, others attend the local junior college, some sign up for trade school, some go into the military, and still others head right into the work force. Adjustments come easy to some, but others take a nosedive into depression, stress, and frustration over what to do with their lives.

I've seen a large number of students graduate from high school into a wilderness stage of life. In particular, they struggle in four major areas.

Friendships

The friends you had in high school may end up being your friends for life. Or maybe not. One thing for certain is this: After high school, friendships change. Your best friend may move across the country to go to a university. You may decide you want to become a logger in the Pacific Northwest and move away from your friends.

If you're afraid of upcoming changes in your friendships after graduation, talk with your friends about what you think life will be like after high school. Talk about what might be different and what might stay the same in your friendship. New jobs, new moves, new interests, and new classes will affect your time schedules and priorities. That's worth talking about. Change is scary when it catches you off guard. That's why you can prepare for it now by realizing it will come. Thank God, the one thing that won't change is His friendship toward you.

Family

Once you graduate from high school, not only does your legal status change (oh, boy, you can either go to war or go to prison), but your family status changes, too. You're no longer just a kid in high school. As soon as the grad night party is over, your parents' expectations may change quickly. You may have to pay rent if you're living at home. You may have to pay for some or all of your college expenses. Taking the family car may not be as easy as it used to be. You will have more time and freedom than you may know what to do with. Your parents may be cool during this transition, but whatever happens, you're no longer in high school. Your role in your family is even more important as you begin to make your own decisions as an adult. It's something to think about.

Finances

If you're like many graduating seniors, you probably haven't taken any financial seminars lately. *It's not too late!* Finances can be one huge headache if you haven't learned how to properly save, spend, and separate your priorities when it comes to cash flow. Gas, car payments, insurance, rent, food, clothes, spending money, books, tuition—you're going to need more money than you did in high school. You could avoid a walletload of problems by learning how to do a budget; figure out how much you're earning, what your expenses are, and what things you'd like to do in the future that require money. Banks don't care if you don't know how to balance your checkbook, but they will take your hard-earned cash for bouncing a check. Avoid unnecessary financial mistakes by not knowing how to handle your moola. It simply costs too much. (Here's a hot tip that'll save you cash: Buy *Financial Self-Defense* by Charles Givens. It's an easy and very informative way to learn how to handle your finances.)

Future

What are you going to do after high school? You'll hear that question a million times. Some students know exactly what they're going to do after high school. Go to college. Work for my dad. Travel the east coast of Africa. But others are clueless about the future. They're still trying to figure out what life will be like without a locker. It's all right not to have everything figured out.

Who knows what you'll be doing five to ten years from now? One person—God. You can breathe easier when you realize that wherever you go, God promises to lead you. He knows and understands the future. All the big decisions and changes you'll be facing are ones He can handle. He wants to be a part of your future. Be sure to keep Him the center of your plans because He's got great ones especially for you. "For I know the thoughts that I think toward you," says the LORD, "thoughts of peace and not of evil, to give you a future and a hope" (Jeremiah 29:11).

Hang in There

(Developing Endurance)

Do you ever feel like you don't know what to say? You find out your best friend's mom has cancer. What do you say? Your dad loses his job. What do you say? What do you say when people come to you with complex problems that don't have easy answers? Sometimes the best thing to say is nothing at all or maybe a simple, "Hang in there." I know it sounds trite and won't solve problems, but it can show others you care.

God's Word is designed to help you hang in there when times are tough because, sometimes, hanging in there is all you can do. The best place to hang is in the arms of God. He will support you; He will give you strength, encouragement, perseverance, courage, and peace. God defies all gravity. He promises never to leave you or forsake you. Never, ever, ever. Hang in there and hang on tight.

Where is God when I wonder if He has the power to help me with my struggles?

Then the Lord knows how to deliver the godly out of temptations (2 Peter 2:9).

Where is God when I've cried out to Him, but He doesn't seem to be listening?
The righteous cry out, and the LORD hears, and delivers them out of all their troubles (Psalm 34:17).

Where is God when I know there are no quick fixes to my problems, but I need help trusting Him to pull me through?
You, who have shown me great and severe troubles, shall revive me again, and bring me up again from the depths of the earth (Psalm 71:20).

Where is God when I can't figure out why He is allowing me to experience problem after problem?
In this you greatly rejoice, though now for a little while, if need be, you have been grieved by various trials, that the genuineness of your faith, being much more precious than gold that perishes, though it is tested by fire, may be found to praise, honor, and glory at the revelation of Jesus Christ (1 Peter 1:6–7).

Where is God when I thought Christians didn't have problems like everyone else? Am I wrong?
Many are the afflictions of the righteous, but the LORD delivers him out of them all (Psalm 34:19).

Where is God when I'm tired of facing my problems alone and I need hope for the future?
For our light affliction, which is but for a moment, is working for us a far more exceeding and eternal weight of glory (2 Corinthians 4:17).

Where is God when I want to know if it's possible to experience His peace in every situation?
Now may the Lord of peace Himself give you peace always in every way. The Lord be with you all (2 Thessalonians 3:16).

I Can't Decide

(Making Decisions)

You face hundreds of decisions each day. That means hundreds of thousands of decisions each year. Multiply that by a lifetime and you've lots of decisions to make. Millions. Possibly gigabillions. The decisions you make, positive or negative, will have a big effect on your life and others' lives. That's why it's very important to know how to make good decisions.

The best thing you could have to help you make good decisions is God's wisdom. God promises to give you wisdom just by asking Him. (See James 1.) He wants to give you everything you need to count the cost in following Him. He's seen too many young people suffer from lousy decision making. That doesn't have to be you! When you feel like you can't decide between following God or following everyone else, take time to think through the consequences of your decision. What will the outcome be? Will your decision hurt or help those you really care about? Does your decision please God or hurt Him? Remember: Bad decisions are cheap, but in the end they cost you a lot. If you follow the flock, you could end up a lamb chop.

Where is God when I wonder if He will give me wisdom to make good decisions?
For the LORD gives wisdom; from His mouth come knowledge and understanding (Proverbs 2:6).

Where is God when I'm confused about who's really in control in making decisions? Me or God?
The lot is cast into the lap, but its every decision is from the LORD (Proverbs 16:33).

Where is God when I've seen so many of my friends suffer from making stupid decisions and I want to show them there's a better way?

Who is wise and understanding among you? Let him show by good conduct that his works are done in the meekness of wisdom (James 3:13).

Where is God when I wonder if I should give money to the church or not?
So let each one give as he purposes in his heart, not grudgingly or of necessity; for God loves a cheerful giver (2 Corinthians 9:7).

Where is God when I wrestle with trying to please Him and my friends? What is the benefit for pleasing God instead of my friends?
Happy is the man who finds wisdom, and the man who gains understanding; for her proceeds are better than the profits of silver, and her gain than fine gold (Proverbs 3:13–14).

Where is God when I've made some bad decisions and suffered the consequences? How do I start over?
Wisdom is the principal thing; therefore get wisdom. And in all your getting, get understanding (Proverbs 4:7).

Where is God when I need help telling a friend why it's important to make good decisions?
Seek good and not evil, that you may live; so the LORD God of hosts will be with you, as you have spoken (Amos 5:14).

Where is God when I want to know how I can always have God's guidance in making wise decisions?
Pray without ceasing (1 Thessalonians 5:17).

Where is God when I sometimes think I won't be affected by making a bad decision?
Do not be deceived, God is not mocked; for whatever a man sows, that he will also reap (Galatians 6:7).

I Hope This Works

(Depending on God)

Have you ever tried to fix a busted engine with the wrong set of tools? Or lift a gigantic piece of furniture up a narrow staircase and try to squeeze it through a teeny, tiny door? Or what about trying to jury-rig a whatchamacallit to a frayed piece of string connected to a questionable thing that used to work a few years ago? Every time you've tried to manipulate, repair, or restore something to work beyond all possibilities, you've joined the praying faithful millions who've suffered under similar situations. People who have tried to fix something when they know it won't work have sung the familiar desperate and halfhearted chorus, "I hope this works."

When people think of religion, prayer, faith, and all the other things concerned with trying to know God better, their approach isn't too different. People think, *Gee, I hope I get to heaven someday. I hope God hears my prayers. I hope this prayer stuff works.*

Hope like that really isn't hope. It's chance. It's trusting in something unreliable and unknowable. The God of the Bible is nothing like that. He is knowable, reliable, trustworthy, listening, caring, compassionate, and loving. He is interested in your life. When you put your hope in Him, you're not trusting in something that may blow up in your face. You're hoping in the One who created hope, the One who has given you hope so you can hope in Him.

Where is God when I'm discouraged and feel like God's never gonna finish what He started in my life?
But now, O LORD, You are our Father; we are the clay, and You our potter; and all we are the work of Your hand (Isaiah 64:8).

Where is God when I don't feel like I'm filled with His hope the way I used to be?
Now may the God of hope fill you with all joy and peace in believing, that you may abound in hope by the power of the Holy Spirit (Romans 15:13).

Where is God when I pray to Him, but I'm never sure if He answers my prayers?
By awesome deeds in righteousness You will answer us, O God of our salvation, You who are the confidence of all the ends of the earth, and of the far-off seas (Psalm 65:5).

Where is God when I'm scared my friends won't trust in Him if I mess up?
Let not those who wait for You, O Lord GOD of hosts, be ashamed because of me; let not those who seek You be confounded because of me, O God of Israel (Psalm 69:6).

Where is God when I put my hope in Him, but I'm impatient waiting for Him?
Therefore I will look to the LORD; I will wait for the God of my salvation; my God will hear me (Micah 7:7).

Where is God when I face disappointment after disappointment? Will God disappoint me like others?
Now hope does not disappoint, because the love of God has been poured out in our hearts by the Holy Spirit who was given to us (Romans 5:5).

Where is God when I lack hope and I need Him to give me some quick?
Now may our Lord Jesus Christ Himself, and our God and Father, who has loved us and given us everlasting consolation and good hope by grace, comfort your hearts and establish you in every good word and work (2 Thessalonians 2:16–17).

Life Doesn't Make Sense

(Figuring Out Life)

Let's get one thing straight: Most of the time, life doesn't make sense. Some people believe life makes sense all the time: There's a concrete explanation for all problems. Other people believe that because life doesn't make sense, it's meaningless, and no one should even attempt to make sense out of the insensible. (Dress code for this group is black.) Still others believe that if everyone would just be positive, listen to the earth's vibrations, meditate, and converge with the lunar tidal pull, the whole world would sing in perfect harmony. *I may be wrong, but I don't think so.*

This life is difficult, it does get confusing, and there are millions of issues, problems, and gray areas that may never be answered . . . in this life. God, who stands in our time zone and outside time itself, is interested in helping you make sense out of life. This life and eternal life. His Word may not give you the exact answer on how to solve environmental waste or explain why both humans and monkeys eat bananas, but it will give you understanding of how to approach life, how to get life, and how to live life in a way that makes sense.

Where is God when I don't understand why some people say such stupid things?
He who is devoid of wisdom despises his neighbor, but a man of understanding holds his peace (Proverbs 11:12).

Where is God when I need help understanding His Word so I can follow Him closer?
Make me understand the way of Your precepts; so shall I meditate on Your wonderful works (Psalm 119:27).

Where is God when I don't understand why there's such an abuse of justice in this world?
Evil men do not understand justice, but those who seek the LORD understand all (Proverbs 28:5).

Where is God when others seem to know so much about this life, but I feel clueless?
I am Your servant; give me understanding, that I may know Your testimonies (Psalm 119:125).

Where is God when I know He's leading my life, but I still feel like I don't know where my life is going?
A man's steps are of the Lord; how then can a man understand his own way? (Proverbs 20:24).

Where is God when I'm overwhelmed by His awesome creation? Is it even possible to understand it all?
As you do not know what is the way of the wind, or how the bones grow in the womb of her who is with child, so you do not know the works of God who makes everything (Ecclesiastes 11:5).

Where is God when my stupid decisions interfere with living the way He wants me to? What should I do?
Therefore do not be unwise, but understand what the will of the Lord is (Ephesians 5:17).

Where is God when I don't understand why my non-Christian friends are puzzled by the importance of my relationship with God?
But the natural man does not receive the things of the Spirit of God, for they are foolishness to him; nor can he know them, because they are spiritually discerned (1 Corinthians 2:14).

Where is God when I want to do the right thing, but I never do what I know is right?
For what I am doing, I do not understand. For what I will to do, that I do not practice; but what I hate, that I do (Romans 7:15).

My Personal Bodyguard

(God's Protection)

Have you ever been beaten up? I mean really worked, pounded in the pavement like a road kill on the highway? Getting beaten up hurts; it causes bleeding, swelling, discoloration of the skin, and a host of other physical deformities. Getting beaten up is humiliating.

It hits an extremely sensitive nerve I think we all fear: being made fun of. Nobody wants to be known as a wimp or a weakling. Who wants to be the center of rejection and ridicule? No one. Not even Jesus. But you know what? Jesus Christ was made fun of. He was ridiculed. He got beaten up. People wanted to put Him in a mental institution. They thought He was crazy, a complete idiot for saying the things He said. Jesus understands what it's like to get worked. He got His body worked to death.

Jesus understands fear. So does His Father. That's why the Bible is filled with verses about protection. God wants to protect you from all sorts of fears: enemies, danger, physical harm, depressing thoughts, the unknown, past sins, ridicule, and humiliation. In a sense, He wants to be your personal bodyguard.

Where is God when I wonder if there's ever going to be a time when I won't have any enemies?
Deliver me from my enemies, O my God; defend me from those who rise up against me (Psalm 59:1).

Where is God when I'm scared to walk to school alone? Will God walk with me?
The LORD will preserve him and keep him alive, and he will be blessed on the earth (Psalm 41:2).

Where is God when I want to have confidence that He is with me in the midst of trouble?
Though I walk in the midst of trouble, You will revive me; You will stretch out Your hand against the wrath of my enemies, and Your right hand will save me (Psalm 138:7).

Where is God when I feel like He's hiding from me and the problem I took to Him? Did David ever feel like that when he was in trouble?
And do not hide Your face from Your servant, for I am in trouble; hear me speedily. Draw near to my soul, and redeem it; deliver me because of my enemies (Psalm 69:17–18).

Where is God when I'm feeling bombarded with temptation, but I doubt if He's really going to protect me?
But the Lord is faithful, who will establish you and guard you from the evil one (2 Thessalonians 3:3).

Where is God when I want to thank Him for protecting me from harm in a car accident?
But let all those rejoice who put their trust in You; let them ever shout for joy, because You defend them; let those also who love Your name be joyful in You (Psalm 5:11).

Where is God when my problems affect my relationship with Him and I need His protection?
Do not withhold Your tender mercies from me, O LORD; let Your lovingkindness and Your truth continually preserve me (Psalm 40:11).

Where is God when I've heard that Jesus actually prayed for His disciples' protection? Is Jesus praying for me?
Now I am no longer in the world, but these are in the world, and I come to You. Holy Father, keep through Your name those whom You have given Me, that they may be one as We are (John 17:11).

Nail Biters Anonymous

(Bad Habits)

My name is Joey, and I'm a nail biter. No toenail biting. Just fingernails. I know, I know, it's gross, and I'm really trying to work on this disgusting problem. You're not the only one who thinks it's foul. It drives my wife crazy. Most of the time, I do it without thinking, but if you're a nail biter like me, you understand. When I was little, I chewed my fingernails raw. Then I stopped for a long time, years even, but somehow, a couple of years ago I started up again.

People who don't have this gross habit say that nail biters are worrywarts. Nail biters are nervous, anxious, or worried about something in the past, present, or future, so they try to take their minds off what they're doing by biting their fingernails. That's me. I do worry about things, lots of things. That's why I'm glad I know God, who cares about what's on my heart. I can give Him my problems. I can trust Him with things I have no control over. I know He wants to replace my worries with peace. And I'm depending on Him to give me the strength to stop biting my fingernails.

Where is God when my nervous habits drive others crazy? Will God help me change?
Be anxious for nothing, but in everything by prayer and supplication, with thanksgiving, let your requests be made known to God (Philippians 4:6).

Where is God when I need His Word to soothe my stress-filled life?
In the multitude of my anxieties within me, Your comforts delight my soul (Psalm 94:19).

Where is God when I know I can't do anything to change the future, but I worry about it all the time?
Therefore do not worry about tomorrow, for tomorrow will worry about its own things. Sufficient for the day is its own trouble (Matthew 6:34).

Where is God when I want Jesus to help me stop worrying about things I have no control over?
And which of you by worrying can add one cubit to his stature? If you then are not able to do the least, why are you anxious for the rest? (Luke 12:25–26).

Where is God when I don't spend much time alone with Him because I'm worried about so many things? Can anyone relate?
And Jesus answered and said to her, "Martha, Martha, you are worried and troubled about many things. But one thing is needed,

and Mary has chosen that good part, which will not be taken away from her" (Luke 10:41–42).

Where is God when I'm so stressed about all my problems that I don't see much growth in my walk with God? Why is this?
Now he who received seed among the thorns is he who hears the word, and the cares of this world and the deceitfulness of riches choke the word, and he becomes unfruitful (Matthew 13:22).

Where is God when I want Him to show me how I can give Him my worries and frustrations?
Search me, O God, and know my heart; try me, and know my anxieties; and see if there is any wicked way in me, and lead me in the way everlasting (Psalm 139:23–24).

Overcoming Adversity

(Tackling Problems)

There's a group at my church called Overcomers. The people involved in Overcomers have, in one way or another, been beaten up by life. Drugs. Sexual abuse. Alcohol. Unhealthy relationships. Addictions. Miserable family relationships. Whatever problem or tragedy you can think of, these people have faced it. That's why they're in Overcomers. They're sick of living life out of a coffin. They don't want to be another statistic, disaster story, or "Rescue 911" fatality. Hitting their problems head-on, admitting they're powerless over their lives, and depending on God to help them make healthy decisions are just a few ways they're rearranging their lives. They refuse to roll over and play dead to their struggles. Their struggles aren't going to win. They are.

Are you an overcomer? If you've realized you can't handle life on your own and you need the help of an almighty, awesome, and ever-loving Father, you're in the process of overcoming. Jesus Christ came to this world to overcome sin, death, tears, pain, and suffering. In Jesus Christ, you can be an overcomer. Who has ever overcome your life with love like that? He promises to give you strength when you're weary, power when you're weak, and hope when you're hopeless. When I'm feeling beaten up and discouraged by my problems, this Bible verse reminds me, regardless of how I'm feeling, that I'm an overcomer in Christ: "He said to me, 'It is done! I am the Alpha and the Omega, the Beginning and the End. I will give of the fountain of the water of life freely to him who thirsts. He who overcomes shall inherit all things, and I will be his God and he shall be My son'" (Revelation 21:6–7).

Where is God when I have so many enemies? What am I supposed to do?
Lest my enemy say, "I have prevailed against him"; lest those who trouble me rejoice when I am moved (Psalm 13:4).

Where is God when I'm afraid of getting beaten up at school?
"They will fight against you, but they shall not prevail against you. For I am with you," says the LORD, "to deliver you" (Jeremiah 1:19).

Where is God when I doubt if He will really help me with my problems?
Jesus said to him, "If you can believe, all things are possible to him who believes" (Mark 9:23).

Where is God when I struggle with making good decisions instead of bad ones?
Do not be overcome by evil, but overcome evil with good (Romans 12:21).

Where is God when I'm having trouble overcoming my fear of failure?
For I, the LORD your God, will hold your right hand, saying to you, "Fear not, I will help you" (Isaiah 41:13).

Where is God when I feel like I'm under constant attack from Satan?
You are of God, little children, and have overcome them, because He who is in you is greater than he who is in the world (1 John 4:4).

Where is God when I feel like a loser and insecure that I'll amount to anything?
For whatever is born of God overcomes the world. And this is the victory that has overcome the world—our faith (1 John 5:4).

Getting Back in the Sandbox

Homework. Three tests on Thursday. *Stress.* After-school sports. "Will the coach put me in Friday night?" A part-time job. "Will I have enough to pay my car insurance?" PSAT exams. "How will I do? I've got to score high to get into college." *Fear.* "There's no way I can get my chores done after school. I'm too busy! I'm going to get killed!" *Worry.* "What am I going to do after high school? What am I going to do with my life?" *Sound familiar?*

Students today are busier than ever, but in the midst of having enough work for three people (let alone one), very few are happy about their frenetic life-styles. Kerry, a senior on our student leadership team with a 4.2 GPA, said to me, "Stress is a major factor in my life." She is very active in student leadership in the youth ministry, is enrolled in Japanese classes at the local junior college and SAT exam courses at a local university, and is a member of the school tennis team, so I can't begin to imagine why stress is a major factor in her life. Can you?

It's time for young people to get back in the sandbox of life to relearn what it's like to have a few hours of good clean fun. Living life on purpose means making playtime a regular priority. I don't mean carving time out of the week to be childish or immature; rather, I mean setting aside consistent, fun-filled times to be child-like. *Recreation* means "to re-create" or, in simpler terms, "to play." Do whatever you love to do: shooting hoops, running with your dog, taking a nap, or hanging out with friends. A key characteristic of a child of God is the ability to play and enjoy God's creation.

Here are some play-filled thoughts on how to hit the turn signal, pull out of the frantic lane, and enjoy the journey of life in the slow lane.

Today . . .

Fly a kite, run in the sprinklers, tickle a child, tell a joke, sleep in, encourage someone, blow a bubble, write a letter, eat a cookie, ride a bike, watch a sunset, dream a dream, release a balloon, give a smile, wipe a tear, light a fire, call home, make a sand castle, sing a song, share a secret, destroy a fear, love someone lonely, play tag, chase a cloud, turn off the TV, go for a swim, finger paint, spread some hope, laugh till it hurts, catch a fish, forget a worry, read a book, say a prayer, nap under a tree, jump a rope, build a fort, lie on the couch, go to the zoo, climb a rock, leave work early, lift a frown, forgive a failure, challenge a doubt, buy a puppy, go out to dinner, brave a defeat, surprise a friend, admit you're wrong, throw a snowball, roll in the leaves, plan a vacation, lick two scoops instead of one, risk an adventure, say, "I love you," play, pick a flower, count the stars, let go of a hurt, think a new thought, wink for no reason, reach out because, invent a new game, go barefoot, walk your cat, breathe easy, rejoice in a gift, live as a child, live like you mean it—not as you wish it, make life a celebration—not a duty, dance with the Giver, live, live on, live today.